Peter Lucantoni

Introduction to

English as a Second Language

Workbook

Fourth edition

CAMBRIDGE
UNIVERSITY PRESS

University Printing House, Cambridge CB2 8BS, United Kingdom

One Liberty Plaza, 20th Floor, New York, NY 10006, USA

477 Williamstown Road, Port Melbourne, VIC 3207, Australia

314–321, 3rd Floor, Plot 3, Splendor Forum, Jasola District Centre,
New Delhi – 110025, India

103 Penang Road, #05-06/07, Visioncrest Commercial, Singapore 238467

Cambridge University Press is part of the University of Cambridge.

It furthers the University's mission by disseminating knowledge in the pursuit of
education, learning and research at the highest international levels of excellence.

www.cambridge.org
Information on this title:
www.cambridge.org/9781107688810 (Paperback)
www.cambridge.org/9781316602980 (Paperback)

First published 2014

20 19 18 17 16 15 14 13 12

Printed in Dubai by Oriental Press

ISBN 978-1-107-68881-0 (Paperback)
ISBN 978-1-316-60298-0 (Paperback)

....

DEDICATION
Many, many thanks to Lydia Kellas for all her wonderful ideas and
interesting suggestions for the activities in this Workbook.

Contents

Menu

Introduction

This *Introduction to English as a Second Language* Workbook supports the Coursebook to form a one-year, theme-based intermediate English course. It is for students who are not yet ready to start a demanding, exam-focused course such as the International General Certificate of Secondary Education (IGCSE) in English as a Second Language (E2L). Once you have completed this intermediate course, you could move on to study the IGCSE Coursebook and accompanying Workbook, which is a two-year exam course that will properly prepare you for the IGCSE E2L examination.

It is assumed that most of you who use this book will be studying English in order to improve your educational or employment prospects, and it, therefore, includes a broad range of topics and themes relevant to this goal. You will find passages and activities based on a wide variety of stimulating cross-curriculum topics and about people from all over the world, which I hope you will enjoy reading and discussing.

This Workbook follows the same procedure as the Coursebook, and is divided into two parts: *The world around us* and *Human endeavour*. Each themed part is sub-divided into units, which focus on topics such as space (Unit 1), natural disasters (Unit 3), explorers (Unit 9) and wonders of the world (Unit 16). Each unit is further divided into three or four sections covering the language skills of vocabulary, grammar, reading and writing.

The content of the Workbook units develops the content of the Coursebook units. It provides you with extra grammar and vocabulary practice, while also giving you more reading and listening texts, as well as opportunities for writing.

I hope you enjoy using this book and I wish you success in your studies!

Peter Lucantoni

Unit 1: How many planets are there in space?

A Vocabulary

1 In Unit 1 of the Coursebook, you read about the planets. How much do you remember? Complete the table using the information in the box. List the planets in increasing distance from the sun.

Earth Jupiter Uranus
Mars Pluto Saturn
Neptune Mercury Venus

4.50 billion km
108 million km
1.43 billion km
2.88 billion km
5.91 billion km
150 million km
228 million km
779 million km
58 million km

Name of the planet in English	Name of god/ goddess, if represented	Name of the planet in your language	Distance of the planet from the sun
Earth	none		150 million km

2 Match the words to the descriptions. Then choose **five** words and use them in sentences of your own. Write them on page 8.

Word	Description
launch (verb)	the sun, planets and moons
mythical	something very small
parachute	imaginary, or not real
planet	a mountain with an opening from which lava comes
classified	a large round mass that orbits a star
solar system	an instrument designed to make distant objects seem closer
desert	the practice of farming
dwarf	arranged in a group according to features
telescope	to send something off into the air
agriculture	a piece of curved transparent material to send out light rays
volcano	an empty, waterless area of land
lens	a cloth canopy that allows something to descend slowly

_____

_____

_____

_____

_____

_____

_____

_____

_____

_____

B Language focus: Passive forms, prefixes, question forms

Passive forms

1 **Tick the sentences below that are in the passive. Then underline the passive verbs.**

   a The planets are named after mythical Greek and Roman gods and goddesses. ☐

   b The planets were given their names thousands of years ago. ☐

   c Yuri Gagarin was a Russian cosmonaut. ☐

   d The space shuttle _Discovery_ launched the Hubble Space Telescope. ☐

2 **Complete the table.**

Tense	Subject	_to be_	Past participle	Final clause
present	images		(produce)	by rays.
past	the planets		(give)	their names.
present perfect	many animals		(send)	into space.
past perfect	most astronauts		(train)	in Russia.
will future	more training		(require)	next year.

3 **Read the following information about light rays and eyesight. As you read, put the verbs in brackets into the correct passive form. Then draw some simple diagrams, based on the information in the text.**

Light rays

Rays **(a)** _____ (*produce*) by light sources. These rays stream out in all directions. When an object **(b)** _____ (*hit*) by a light ray, the ray usually bounces off. If light rays enter our eyes, we see either the source of the light, or the object that reflected the rays towards us. The angle of the rays gives the object its apparent size.

Eyesight

Light rays from an object **(c)** _____ (*bend*) by the lens of the eye. An image **(d)** _____ (*form*) by the lens on the light-sensitive retina of the eye, and then this image **(e)** _____ (*change*) into a message that travels to the brain. The image is upside down on the retina, but the brain 'sees' it as upright.

Adapted from *The Way Things Work* by David Macaulay (DK Limited, 1988).

Prefixes

4 **Complete this definition of a prefix.**

A prefix is a letter or g _ _ _ _ of letters placed at the b _ _ _ _ _ _ _ _ of a word to change its m _ _ _ _ _ _ .

5 **You saw the words below in the Coursebook. What prefixes make them into different words?**

a _ _ _ covered

b _ _ _ _ scopes

c _ _ _ _ _ world

d _ _ _ _ metres

e _ _ _ _ _ mit

f _ _ harmed

g _ _ hydrated

6 **Look at these words. Underline the prefix in each one. What does each prefix mean?**

a astronaut

_____

b cosmonaut

_____

c telescope

_____

d agriculture

_____

e unscramble

_____

7 **Look at these five prefixes. What do they mean? For each prefix, think of two words and then use them in complete sentences in your notebook.**

a trans

b micro

c super

d sub

e tech

_____

_____

_____

_____

Question forms

8 You came across Yuri Gagarin in the Coursebook. Complete the questions about him.

Example: Who … ?
Who was Yuri Gagarin?
He was a cosmonaut.

a What _____?

Vostok 1.

b Which _____?

He came from the USSR.

c Where _____?

Round the earth.

d Why _____?

Because he was the first man in space.

e How _____?

He jumped out of his spacecraft and used his parachute.

f When _____?

On 12th April 1961.

9 Have you heard of Felix Baumgartner – or 'Fearless Felix' as he is sometimes known? Felix jumped from a spacecraft and then used his parachute to reach Earth! Read the text, then write questions and answers using the information given.

Example: Who …?
Who was Felix Baumgartner?
He was an Austrian space skydiver.

Felix Baumgartner, an Austrian space skydiver, also known as 'Fearless Felix', made a giant leap from 38 kilometres above Earth on 14th October 2012. A new world record was made when he carried out the highest jump using only his body. During the jump, he spent three minutes and 43 seconds just falling, reaching speeds of more than 1357.6 kph, before opening his parachute and landing in the desert in New Mexico. In total, the jump lasted eight minutes and eight seconds. Around 52 million people around the world watched the jump.

a What _____?

_____

b Which _____?

_____

c Where _____?

_____

d Why _____?

_____

e How _____?

_____

f When _____?

_____

C Reading and writing

1 **Read this text about astronomy in China. As you read, complete the gaps using the time references given.**

At a later date	during the years 25–220 CE	in the 17th century
~~in the 4th century BCE~~	thousands of years ago	

Astronomy in China has a very long history: detailed records of astronomical observations began **(a)** _in the 4th century BCE_ and **(b)** _____, Chinese astronomy was influenced by both Indian and Islamic astronomy. **(c)** _____ , **(d)** _____ , the telescope was introduced, which brought Chinese astronomy into the modern world.

Unlike western astronomy, which uses the mythical names of Roman and Greek gods and goddesses to name the planets, the Chinese planets got their names **(e)** _____ from ancient Chinese astronomy. They are named after the five elements. Mercury: water, Venus: metal/gold, Mars: fire, Jupiter: wood and Saturn: fire, 'Earth' means 'land sphere'.

Unlike the solar system in the western world, Chinese astronomy has five 'true' planets, which are called 'moving stars'.

2 **Use the notes below to write a paragraph about the planet Venus, which is sometimes called the 'Morning Star'.**

Venus = brightest object in sky, except for sun and moon.

Called 'Morning Star' when appears in east at dawn.

Called 'Evening Star' when in west at dusk.

Thousands of years ago, evening star called Hesperus, morning star Phosphorus.

Because of distance of Venus and Earth from sun, Venus never visible more than three hours before dawn, three hours after dusk.

Difficult to study from Earth because covered in clouds.

Got most knowledge from space vehicles.

Very powerful radar on *Magellan* spacecraft found huge active volcanoes on Venus.

Unit 2: What's a living creature?

A Vocabulary

1 Look at the following words. Choose **two** synonyms for each.

Words	Synonyms
spotted	briefly
	drift
identified	findings
	hang
temporarily	recognised
	rejected
float	saw
	unusual
rare	detections
	fly
sightings	glide
	momentarily
denied	noticed
	refused
hover	uncommon
	understood

2 Two of the words in Activity A1 have very similar meanings. Write the words next to the definitions below.

a Remain in one place in the air. _____

b Rest on the surface of a liquid without sinking. _____

B Language focus: Adverbs, word building, 'signpost' words

Adverbs

1 Which of the following words are adverbs? Underline them.

> apparently   carefully   wonderful   increasingly   lovely   good
> always   quickly   never   beautify   apply   several

2 Complete the sentences using an appropriate adverb from Activity B1.

a Christina opened the gift very _____ .

b Elephants are _____ being killed for their tusks.

c Sami wasn't at school today. _____ he wasn't feeling well.

d Teachers _____ hand out the examination papers until all the students are silent.

e Fatima _____ finished her lunch, then started her homework.

f We _____ have an end-of-year party at school.

Word building

3 Build new words from the list below.

Example: *satisfy (verb): satisfaction (noun), satisfying/satisfied (adjectives)*

a health (noun)   _____

b fertility (noun)   _____

c produce (verb)   _____

d energise (verb)   _____

e reproduction (noun)   _____

f sensitive (adjective)   _____

g respond (verb)   _____

h grow (verb)   _____

4 Use a word from Activity B3 to complete the sentences opposite.

Example: *He had a very **satisfying** meal at the new restaurant.*

a They used to have a _____ lifestyle, but now they eat too much fast food.

b I asked the teacher for help, but her _____ wasn't very clear.

c Dario went for a very _____ walk and felt much better.

d Claire, the new manager, has increased the level of _____ at the factory.

e The land near the river is very _____ and excellent for growing crops.

f The _____ cycle of a bird is different from a mammal's.

g Nicolas never speaks very _____ . He upsets people very easily.

h The _____ rate is rising steadily.

'Signpost' words

5 Put the 'signpost' words below in the appropriate column of the table.

When	Contrast	In addition
	although	

```
also    although    and
but     even though
finally    firstly
furthermore
however    lastly
on the other hand
or    secondly    so
```

C Reading

1 Look at this newspaper headline. What is the missing word?

At 13,000 years, _____ is world's oldest organism.

2 Quickly read the newspaper article to check your answer.

[1] It began life during the last ice age, long before man turned to agriculture and built the first cities in the fertile crescent of the Middle East. It was already thousands of years old when the Egyptians built their pyramids and the ancient Britons erected Stonehenge.

[2] The Jurupa oak tree first sprouted into life when much of the world was still covered in glaciers. It has stood on its windswept hillside in southern California for at least 13,000 years, making it the oldest known living organism, according to a study published today.

[3] Scientists believe that the tree, composed of a sprawling community of cloned bushes, is the oldest living thing because it has repeatedly renewed itself to ensure its survival through successive periods of drought, frost, storms and high winds.

[4] This single Jurupa oak extends nearly 23 metres and is extremely slow growing. The scientists said that it could only have got this big by clonal growth, re-sprouting from the roots following wildfires. After a while, the centre of the colony degrades, leaving the haphazard collection of stems visible today.

[5] 'Ring counts show that the Jurupa oak is growing extremely slowly. At its current rate of about one-twentieth of an inch [of growth] per year, it would have taken at least 13,000 years for the clone to reach its current size. And it could be much older,' said Michael May, a member of the research team.

The scientists believe the oak began life in a far colder climate during the last ice age, said Andrew Saunders, a member of the team. 'This literally appears to be the last living remnant of a vanished woody vegetation that occupied the inland valleys at the height of the last ice age,' he said.

Adapted from www.independent.co.uk

3 In the Coursebook, you looked at the words opposite as basic characteristics of living things. Tick the characteristics that are mentioned in the article on page 13. Then write the paragraph number that each one appears in.

a movement ☐ _____

b nutrition ☐ _____

c excretion ☐ _____

d reproduction ☐ _____

e sensitivity ☐ _____

f respiration ☐ _____

g growth ☐ _____

4 Read the text again, then put these events into the correct chronological (time) order by numbering them.

a The Britons erected Stonehenge. ☐

b The first cities were built. ☐

c The pyramids were built. ☐

d The last ice age. ☐

e The Jurupa oak tree sprouted into life. ☐

f Man turned to agriculture. ☐

5 Are the following statements true or false? Correct the false sentences.

a All areas of the Middle East were fertile.

_____

b California was covered in ice.

_____

c There are other organisms that are older than the Jurupa oak.

_____

d Drought, frost, storms and high winds killed off the original Jurupa oak.

_____

e The Jurupa oak grows from one central root.

_____

f The Jurupa oak could be older than 13,000 years.

_____

g The Jurupa oak stands amongst other woody vegetation from the same period.

_____

D Reading and writing

1   Quickly read the article.

Can jumbo elephants really paint?

Is it true that elephants are artists? Can they really paint pictures of flowers, trees and even other elephants? Are they the only animals on Earth, apart from human beings, that can create pictorial images?

Last summer my friend, the scientist Richard Dawkins, asked me to look at a video clip on the Internet, taken in Thailand, that showed a young female elephant called Hong painting a picture of an elephant running along, holding a flower in its trunk. He wanted to know if I thought it was a fake.

I was amazed and puzzled by what I saw and decided that I really must find out more. Back in the 1950s, I had myself made a serious study of the artistic abilities of chimpanzees, but they had never achieved anything like this.

Adapted from www.dailymail.co.uk

2   The newspaper article goes on to make the following points:

- The elephants used to work in forests with loggers, which is now illegal.
- The elephants now live in a sanctuary because they can't go back to the wild.
- The elephants 'paint' pictures for tourists, who buy the paintings.
- The keeper secretly guides the elephant by pulling its ear.
- The elephant always produces the same picture.
- The painting produced is a trick, but a clever trick, as the elephant interprets the message from its ear to activate its trunk.

Continue the newspaper article, using the points above. Make sure you connect the sentences carefully and meaningfully.

_____

_____

_____

_____

_____

_____

_____

_____

_____

_____

15

Unit 3: What's a hurricane?

A Vocabulary

1 Hidden in the word snake are **ten** words for natural disasters with all the vowels removed. What are they?

hlstrmvlnchfldtsnmmdslddrghtrthqktrndhrrcnsndstrm

a _____   f _____

b _____   g _____

c _____   h _____

d _____   i _____

e _____   j _____

2 Match each word from Activity A1 with one of the definitions below.

a A prolonged period of abnormally low rainfall. _____

b A strong wind in a desert carrying clouds of sand. _____

c An overflow of a large amount of water over dry land. _____

d Heavy frozen rain falling in showers. _____

e A severe storm with a violent wind. _____

f A tidal wave caused by an earthquake or other disturbance.

_____

g A violent rotating wind storm. _____

h A mass of snow and ice falling rapidly down a mountainside.

_____

i A sudden violent shaking of the ground, caused by movements in the earth's crust. _____

j A rapid movement of a large mass of mud formed from loose soil and water. _____

3 Look at the words in the left-hand column of the table. Find and <u>underline an antonym</u> and ⟨circle a synonym⟩ for each word in the right-hand column. The first one has been done as an example.

drought	various <u>abundance</u> catastrophe ⟨lack⟩
awesome	colourful impressive rapid disappointing
freedom	conformity chance liberty monarchy
destruction	construction ruin build collapse
active	lively passive slow sluggish
light	weight visual heavy weightless
progress	retreat development move revolve
last	continue perish downfall continuity
calm	rugged smooth peaceful agitated
wealth	riches poverty money land
brave	courageous cowardly ambitious frighten
trust	believe distrust push truth

B Language focus: Abstract nouns, conditionals and *if*

Abstract nouns

1 Change the following sentences so that they each use an abstract noun.

Example: *The garden was a <u>beautiful place</u>. The garden was a place of <u>beauty</u>.*

a She angrily stormed out of the room.

She stormed out of the room in _____ .

b He confidently finished his exam.

He finished his exam with _____ .

c The soldiers courageously stood their ground.

The soldiers stood their ground with _____ .

d The mouse saw the dangerous cat.

The mouse saw the _____ in the cat.

e They enjoyed eating the meal.

The meal was eaten with _____ .

f The prisoners rushed towards the border and were free.

The prisoners rushed towards the border and achieved _____ .

g He knows a lot about his subject.

His _____ of the subject is vast.

Conditionals and *if*

2 Rearrange these words to make correct sentences.

a warning signs in an avalanche area if you are take notice of

_____

b try to get in the path if you are caught to the side of it of an avalanche

_____

c try to by an avalanche hit swim with it if you are

_____

d hide approaches in if a basement hurricane the

_____

e power cables on boat be a broken careful of if you live

_____

3 Correct the mistakes in the verb tenses in these sentences.

a If you will see an eruption, will warn others.

_____

b If you saw buildings shaking, moved to an open area.

_____

c If you would walk in an avalanche area, never to travel alone.

_____

d If you can't to avoid an avalanche, trying to hold on to something solid.

_____

e If you have lived in a mobile home, moving out if danger is approaching.

_____

C Reading

1 The passage below talks about the 'Americas' and the 'Caribbean'. Name three countries in the Americas and three in the Caribbean.

Americas	Caribbean

2 Look at the countries below and write them in the correct region. Are any of them the same as the ones you listed in Activity C1?

> Trinidad and Tobago   Brazil   Guyana
> Jamaica   Mexico   The United States
> The Bahamas   Bermuda   Canada
> Alaska   Chile   Peru

The Americas
The Caribbean

3 Read the text at the top of page 19 and find the answers to the questions.

a Why do hurricanes have names?

_____

b How are the names chosen?

_____

c How often are names chosen?

_____

d What kind of names are chosen?

_____

e Are all hurricanes given names?

_____

How do hurricanes get their names?

Names have been given to Atlantic hurricanes for a few hundred years. People living in the Caribbean named storms after the saint of the day on which the hurricane occurred, such as 'Hurricane San Felipe'.

Later on, the latitude–longitude position of a storm's formation was used as a name, but these were difficult to remember and errors were often made.

During the Second World War, military meteorologists working in the Pacific began to use women's names for storms. That naming method made communication so easy that, once this practice started, hurricane names quickly became part of common language and public awareness of hurricanes increased dramatically.

From 1978, meteorologists in the Eastern North Pacific and the Atlantic Ocean began using men's names. For each year, a list of 21 names, each starting with a different letter of the alphabet, was developed and arranged in alphabetical order (names beginning with the letters Q, U, X, Y and Z were not used). The first tropical storm of the year was given the name beginning with the letter 'A', the second with the letter 'B', and so on through the alphabet. During even-numbered years, men's names were given to the odd-numbered storms and, during odd-numbered years, women's names were given to odd-numbered storms. If there are more than 21 named storms in a year, as there were in 2005, the rest of the storms are named according to letters in the Greek alphabet.

The only change that is made to the list of Atlantic hurricane names is the occasional retirement of a name. This is done when a hurricane causes so much death and destruction that reuse of the same name would be insensitive to the people who suffered losses.

Adapted from http://geology.com

4   **Are the following statements true or false?**

a   The tradition of naming hurricanes has occurred for many years.
_____

b   The latitude–longitude system was ineffective. _____

c   Using names made the system efficient and easy. _____

d   People became more interested in hurricanes. _____

e   An additional alphabet was used in some years. _____

f   Men's and women's names were used equally. _____

g   People would relate to hurricanes if they had been badly affected by them. _____

h   A new list is drafted each year. _____

D   Reading and writing

1   **Read the newspaper article on page 20 about Sri Lanka, then answer the questions.**

a   Are the floods the worst that Sri Lanka has ever experienced?

_____

b   Is more heavy rain forecast?

_____

Sri Lanka braces for more floods

[1] After more than a week of heavy rains in Sri Lanka, many people are reported missing, with thousands displaced and more than 17,000 people housed in 100 relief camps.

[2] The Meteorological Department forecasts heavy rains to continue for another week,

[3] Around half of the country's 71 main reservoirs are overflowing and their sluice gates have had to be opened, making the flood situation even worse.

[4] The floods have inundated a number of large towns and rural areas, forcing hospitals to evacuate patients and roads to close after landslides.

[5] The floods are some of the worst that Sri Lanka has seen since early 2011, when unusually heavy monsoon rains left at least 64 people dead and drove more than 1 million people out of their homes.

Adapted from www.abc.net.au

---

2 How is the newspaper article organised? Match the information a–e below with a paragraph from the article.

a Effect on buildings and routes ☐

b Prediction ☐

c Other occurrence ☐

d Immediate impact ☐

e Present supply of water ☐

3 Look at the newspaper article again and find words that mean:

a seven days _____

b evacuated _____

c predicts _____

d artificial lakes _____

e forced _____

---

4 Imagine that, after reading the newspaper article, you did some further research about water in Sri Lanka, then wrote the notes below. Use your notes to write a short article (60–80 words) for your school magazine or newspaper.

Water in Sri Lanka

Charities – give equipment for cleaning dirty water

Equipment – removes bacteria, dirt, but not salt

Also give people tanks to collect rain from monsoon

Project to dig more wells for water

Already some wells giving clean drinking water

Many people survive on only 3 litres per day

Water from wells often has strange taste

Wells can be expensive to set up

Major regional problems – drought and floods

_____

_____

_____

_____

_____

_____

_____

_____

_____

_____

_____

_____

_____

_____

_____

Unit 4: Are there any monsters in the ocean?

A Vocabulary

1 Choose suitable adjectives from the left-hand column to describe the nouns on the right. There may be several possible answers.

Example: *gigantic + insects*

Adjectives	Nouns
volcanic	asteroid
herbivorous	insects
carnivorous	measurement
evaporating	dinosaur
flowering	sea
extinct	mammal
continuous	ocean
metric	reptile
gigantic	sea
descending	reef
shallow	plant

2 Complete these two sentences.

a In the metric system, units _____ than a metre have _____ prefixes.

b In the metric system, units _____ than a metre have _____ prefixes.

3 Write these words in the correct box.

decametre   kilometre   ~~millimetre~~   centimetre
hectometre   decimetre

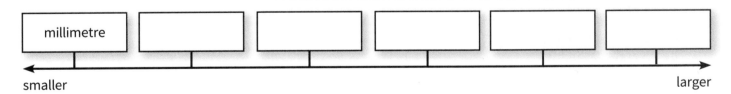

millimetre						

smaller   larger

4 Complete these sentences.

a A metre equals 10 _____ .

b A _____ equals 10 metres.

c A _____ equals 1000 metres.

d A metre equals 1000 _____ .

5 Write a word or phrase with a similar meaning to each of the words in a–f opposite.

a typical _____

b difference _____

c older _____

d smaller _____

e important _____

f largest _____

6 Complete these sentences using a suitable word from Activity A5.

a What do you think is the _____ between fresh water and sea water?

b If you evaporate water from a _____ lake, you would get about 0.15 grams of salt.

c The world's oceans are split up into a number of _____ oceans and seas (which are usually _____).

d The Pacific Ocean is the _____ body of water known to humans.

e Life within our oceans is far _____ than life on land.

B Language focus: Prepositional verbs, past and past perfect tenses

Prepositional verbs

1 Make **six** prepositional verbs by matching each verb with the correct preposition. There may be several possibilities for some of the verbs. Below the table, write what each prepositional verb means.

Verbs	Prepositions
believe	about
look	about
talk	after
wait	for
worry	in
concentrate	on
drive	through

Example: *believe + in = have trust, confidence in*

a _____   **d** _____

b _____   **e** _____

c _____   **f** _____

2 Use the prepositional verbs in Activity B1 in sentences of your own.

Example: *Julia's parents* ***believe in*** *her abilities to be successful in life.*

a _____

b _____

c _____

d _____

e _____

f _____

Past simple and past perfect tenses

3 Fill in the gaps in the text on the right. Three of the words are given in the box below, but you will need to think of the other five yourself.

implied   phrase
time reference

We use the **past simple** tense with a _____ for past

_____ , states and facts, and for _____ past actions.

Sometimes, the time reference may be _____ , i.e. it is

given somewhere else, for example in a _____ sentence or

_____ .

The **past perfect** tense is used to talk about an _____ that

happened _____ another event in the past.

4 Complete the sentences by putting the verbs in brackets into the correct tense (past simple or past perfect). Sometimes either tense is possible.

a   Michelle only _____ (*understand*) the film because she
_____ (*read*) the book.

b   Mark _____ (*know*) the city so well because he _____
(*visit*) it several times before.

c   Harry never _____ (*go*) to a live football match before last
weekend.

d   Chrystalla _____ (*visit*) her friends' home just once while she
was studying at university.

e   Lorna _____ (*apply*) for the part-time job she saw advertised
last week.

f   My brother _____ (*cook*) dinner for me when I _____
(*get*) home last night.

g   Justin and Greg _____ (*finish*) their homework only two minutes
before the doorbell _____ (*ring*).

h   Zak knew he _____ (*need*) glasses before he _____
(*have*) his eyes checked.

C Reading

1 You are going to read a text about deserts. Skim the text and find how many times the words *desert* and *deserts* are used.

Deserts everywhere

[1] Deserts cover about one-seventh of the earth's land surface and 35% of its total surface. Deserts have been classified into sub-tropical deserts, cold winter deserts and cool coastal deserts. Sub-tropical deserts lie between 15° and 30° latitude. They are centred along the Tropics of Cancer and Capricorn.

[2] Deserts are land areas or regions that receive little rain. They are cold at night, and since the desert air is dry, it holds little moisture. Desert regions receive an average annual precipitation of less than 250 millimetres of rain.

[3] A desert, despite being a vast area of land that is extremely dry, with little or no vegetation, comprises one of the major ecosystems on this planet. It supports a wide range of plant and animal species that are attuned to survive in the harsh conditions.

Major sub-tropical deserts

[4] Sahara Desert: The Sahara, the largest desert in the world, occupies an area of 8,600,000 square kilometres and covers almost the whole of North Africa. It is bounded on the west by the Atlantic Ocean, to the north by the Atlas range of mountains and the Mediterranean, and to the east by the Red Sea. To the south is a vast zone of unmoving sand dunes.

[5] Arabian Desert: Occupying almost the whole of the Arabian Peninsula, and covering an area of about 2,300,000 square kilometres, the desert is spread across Saudi Arabia. To its south and south-west is Yemen; Oman lies on its eastern edge; Jordan in the north-west; and the United Arab Emirates and Qatar form its northern limit along with the southern coastline of the Persian Gulf.

[6] Great Sandy Desert: A vast wasteland in the north of Western Australia, the Great Sandy Desert extends from Eighty Mile Beach on the Indian Ocean eastward into Northern Territory, and from Kimberley Downs southward to the Tropic of Capricorn and the Gibson Desert.

Adapted from www.mapsofworld.com

2 All the information below is incorrect. Read the text again and correct the information.

a Earth's land surface is about 35% desert.

_____

b Deserts are centred along the Tropics of Cancer and Capricorn.

_____

c Desert air is very moist.

_____

d Deserts contain vast amounts of vegetation.

_____

e The Sahara Desert has many moving sand dunes.

_____

f The Arabian Desert covers the whole of the Arabian Peninsula.

_____

g The Great Sandy Desert is located in the north of Australia.

_____

3 Match the words and phrases from the text with the correct meaning

Word or phrase from text	Meaning
precipitation	being without vegetation
vegetation	hills of sand
dunes	plants in general
harsh conditions	rain, snow or hail
attuned to survive	adapted to live

4 Re-read paragraph 5 in the reading text. As you read, find all the countries and places on a map.

D Writing

1 Write a sentence using the word *hot* in three different ways, with the following meanings.

a very spicy _____

_____

b successful _____

_____

c knowledgeable _____

_____

2 You are going to write about a 31-man Australian team that explored Antarctica between 1912 and 1914. Of the 31 men, only two had been to Antarctica before, and many had never even seen snow! They took 38 dogs, but only two survived the harsh conditions. The men divided into different groups. Douglas Mawson led one of these groups with Belgrave Ninnis and Xavier Metz.

Use the notes to write the story, using conjunctions and putting the verbs into the correct past tenses. Replace and add words where necessary to form complete, correct sentences. An example is given to start you off.

Start out 10th November 1912 – take Far Eastern route.

Things initially go well – cover 478 kilometres in 35 days.

Disaster strikes – Belgrave Ninnis, likeable 25-year-old, falls down crevasse with two dogs.

For three hours other men call for him – no reply.

Not only lose a man and dogs, also some very important supplies.

Quickly pitch spare tent – make decision to return to base.

Over next few days make good progress – slowly dogs can no longer pull sledge.

8th January Douglas Mawson – only survivor of team – due to harsh conditions.

Has to rush the last 160 kilometres – ship to take him home – arriving 15th January.

Misses ship by five hours – sees it sailing away.

Seen by group of six men – stayed behind to look for his team.

Have to stay in Antarctica another ten months before ship arrives – takes them home.

Mawson finally arrives home February 1914.

Later becomes university professor – two more Antarctic expeditions.

Example: *Douglas Mawson, Belgrave Ninnis and Xavier Metz started out on their Antarctica expedition on 10th November 1912 …*

_____

_____

_____

_____

_____

_____

_____

_____

_____

_____

Unit 5: What's an ecosystem?

A Vocabulary

1 In the Coursebook, you read about the world's different biomes. What are the **six** biomes?

a M _ _ _ _ _ _ _ _ _ _

b M _ _ _ _ _ _ _ _ _ _ _ _

c A _ _ _

d P _ _ _ _

e T _ _ _ _ _ _ _

f T _ _ _ _ _ _ _ _

2 **Complete the definitions. Then match each one to a type of biome above (a–f).**

a High and low-altitude areas where the energy from the sun is _____ enough for water to freeze and create pack ice and ice sheets. ☐

b A region characterised by a severe _____ of available water. ☐

c The climate is characterised by warm to hot, dry summers and _____ to cool, wet winters. ☐

d Found in the lower latitudes with temperatures around 80° F. Very high _____ and little change in seasons. ☐

e A difficult place for plants to live. It is windy, cold and the sunlight at these high altitudes is very _____ . ☐

f A clear four _____ with high rainfall and home to many plants, animals and insects. ☐

3 Complete the crossword. All the words can be found in Unit 5 of the Coursebook.

Clues

Across

1 A food made of liquid (4)

5 All the plants and animals of a particular area (9)

9 A living thing that uses its roots and photosynthesis to survive (5)

10 An animal that feeds on meat (9)

11 A part added on to the end of a word (6)

12 An animal that can feed on both plants and meat (8)

Down

2 A word, letter or number placed before another (6)

3 Very large (4)

4 An animal that feeds on plants (9)

6 A command (10)

7 Vegetation consisting of plants with long, narrow leaves (5)

8 Wheat or other cereal grown for food (5)

B Use of English: Prefixes and suffixes, imperatives for instructions

Prefixes and suffixes

1 Match the prefixes and suffixes to their meanings. Then write a word for each one and say what it means.

Prefix	Meaning	Suffix	Meaning
anti-	opposite	-ment	more than one
de-	not	-less	having characteristics of
dis-	against	-s	without
mis-	wrong	-able/-ible	action or process
non-	half	-ness	state or condition
semi-	not, opposite	-ic	can be done

Example: *anti- = against*
　　　　　antidote = remedy/cure

Prefixes

_____

_____

_____

_____

_____

_____

Suffixes

_____

_____

_____

_____

_____

_____

2 Choose **three** words with prefixes and **three** words with suffixes from Activity B1. Then use the words in sentences of your own.

Example: *The scientists found an antidote for the disease.*

_____

_____

_____

_____

_____

Imperatives for instructions

3 Complete the following explanation about imperatives.

The imperative is used to give an

(a) _____ , a warning or a

(b) _____ . It is formed by using the

(c) _____ verb without *to*, and

without a **(d)** _____ .

4 **Write a set of instructions for making a desert ecosystem for a lizard. Use the words and phrases below to help you.**

a First / read / research / type of lizard / you / want / live / in desert ecosystem

b Next / buy / everything / need: lizard tank, rocks, sand, heat lamp, heat pad, water bowl, lizard

c Then / place / heat pad / under / tank

d Make sure / aquarium / in / safe place / where / won't get knocked over

e After that / pour / sand / tank

f Next / place / rocks / tank

g Position / water bowl / tank

h Finally / place / heat lamp / so / heat / only one side / tank

i Gently / put / lizard / new home

_____

_____

_____

_____

_____

_____

_____

_____

_____

_____

_____

_____

_____

_____

_____

C Reading and writing

1 **Read these posts from internet sites where people talk about their experiences of working with wild animals. Then answer the questions opposite.**

'I got lots of different experiences and so many different impressions about life and work in an organisation that works with people and cares for animals. I can recommend this project to everyone who loves nature and animals, and enjoys working with people. I promise you, you'll have a great time!'

Adapted from www.travellersworldwide.com

'I would definitely recommend this work placement to anyone who has a passion for wildlife and caring for animals, and who does not mind hard work and getting dirty. I would also recommend this to anyone who wishes to have work experience that is very manual and has many opportunities for working outside.'

Adapted from www.travellersworldwide.com

'A great experience if you want hard work because it's not a holiday. I love working with animals and being outside, but was surprised by the level of hard work, and found working with some animals quite traumatic when they arrived hurt or orphaned. So be prepared and accept that it is not going to be an easy holiday.'

a What do all the stories have in common?

_____

b Which story is different and why?

_____

c What sort of place do you think these people worked at?

_____

d What sort of animals do you think they worked with?

_____

e Would you like to do something like this? Why, or why not?

_____

2   **Read this advertisement for volunteers to work at an animal sanctuary in Spain.**

Animal welfare volunteers needed

Do you care about donkeys and mules? Do you have any practical experience or are you keen to learn, and have a little time to spare? We are looking for volunteers to be our 'extra eyes' by regularly following up welfare complaints and investigations, as well as giving advice and support to many donkey and mule owners. As you can imagine, trying to cover the whole of the country takes a lot of manpower, and so the more help we can get, the better life could be for the donkeys and mules.

To give you an idea of what is involved, here are the main areas we need help with:

- Visiting markets, fairs and festivals in your area – taking photos, reporting on any possible cruelty, abuse or illegal trading.

- Visiting possible welfare cases – sometimes we receive welfare complaints that are too far away for us to check in time. If the call is in your area, we will contact you and ask you to gather basic information, such as photos, situation of the donkey, possible owners.

- Checking potential Loan Homes, where people loan donkeys or mules as pets from us. Visit our Loan Homes three times a year to make sure everything is OK and give support and advice to Loan Carers.

If you think you could help us with any of these projects, please contact us for more details: refdelburrito@mail.info

Adapted from www.elrefugiodelburrito.com

Write an email, offering to help as a volunteer at the animal sanctuary. In your email, include the following information:

- your age and which school you go to
- the experience you have (or would like to get) with animals
- when you are available to volunteer
- why you think you would be suitable as a volunteer.

Also ask questions to obtain the following information:

- the exact location of the animal sanctuary
- the days and hours when they need volunteers.

Write about 100 words.

Unit 6: Can bees scare elephants?

A Vocabulary

1 Write a short description of each of these animals. Say if each one is a mammal, reptile, arthropod, bird, amphibian or insect and give an extra piece of information about it.

> bear   cat   chicken   ~~cow~~   dolphin
> fly   frog   human   mouse   rabbit
> shark   sheep   spider   wolf
> bird   arthropod   amphibian

Example: *cow – A large mammal that provides milk to humans.*

_____

_____

_____

_____

_____

_____

_____

_____

_____

2 Complete the puzzle using eight words in red from the text on page 54 in your Coursebook (*Twenty Thousand Leagues Under the Sea*). If you complete the puzzle correctly, you will find another word from this text under the arrow.

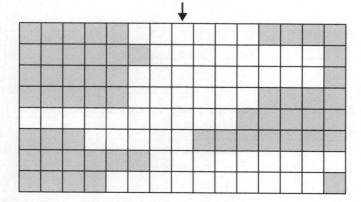

3 Match the words to make **five** phrases from the same text as Activity A2. Be careful – one of the phrases needs three words!

Example: *sea monster*

> biologist   creator   down   electrically
> enigmatic   liner   marine   ~~monster~~
> noted   ocean   powered   ~~sea~~   track

a _____

b _____

c _____

d _____

e _____

4 Choose **eight** words or phrases from Activities A2 and A3 above and use them in sentences of your own.

a _____

b _____

c _____

d _____

e _____

f _____

g _____

h _____

5   What are the _mal-_ words?

a   An illness contracted from mosquitoes is _____ .

b   If a machine does not work properly, it _____ .

c   A person who is not happy is called a _____ .

d   Something with a strange shape is _____ .

e   A _____ act is harmful to other people or animals.

B   Language focus: Infinitives and _-ing_ forms after verbs, question tags

Infinitives and _-ing_ forms after verbs

1   Complete the sentences with the correct form of the verb.

a   Konrad admitted _____ (_take_) the money.

b   Ravinder said that she and her family had enjoyed _____ (_eat_) at the new restaurant.

c   Joshua agreed _____ (_help_) his father paint the kitchen.

d   Otis narrowly avoided _____ (_hit_) the tree.

e   Cho and Rebekah arranged _____ (_meet_) at the cinema.

f   Rae denied _____ (_take_) Yvonne's CDs.

g   Shelly was asked _____ (_not speak_) so loudly.

h   They can't afford _____ (_go_) on holiday this summer.

i   They decided _____ (_not walk_) because of the bad weather.

j   Satish failed _____ (_understand_) the equation in his maths lesson.

2   Look at the following verbs. Which ones are followed by _to_ + infinitive, and which ones by _-ing_?

fail learn manage miss need promise recommend refuse suggest want

to + infinitive	-ing

31

3 Choose **five** verbs from Activity B2 and use them in complete sentences, similar to the ones in Activity B1.

a _____

b _____

c _____

d _____

e _____

4 Read the story. Put the verbs in brackets into the correct form.

I have to admit that one of my most memorable trips abroad was to South Africa. I went
(a) _____ (study) elephants and their response to the sound that bees make. I had
(b) _____ (decide) before I went if I was going **(c)** _____ (refuse) another job offer that I had received. In the other job, I would have been working with a local vet. I remember
(d) _____ (ask) the vet if I could go abroad while I was working with him. He agreed
(e) _____ (give) me the time off until I returned **(f)** _____ (work). But the cute little animals at the vet's, as gorgeous as they were, and as much as I still miss
(g) _____ (hold) and **(h)** _____ (cuddle) them, were not making my career interesting. So I promised myself
(i) _____ (go) on my trip and I managed
(j) _____ (travel) to South Africa the following month. I would recommend
(k) _____ (work) with elephants to anyone who wants to do something completely different. There is plenty of time in life to work with cute little animals, but working with elephants in the wild is something very special. It is something that all of us needs
(l) _____ (do) at some point.

Question tags

5 Use one of the question tags in the box to complete each of the phrases.

> are they?   are you?   aren't they?
> do they?   have they?

a These invertebrates are special, _____

b You're not serious, _____

c Jellyfish and worms have no eyes _____

d Spiders are not insects, _____

e Nobody has ever seen a living giant squid,

_____

6 Complete these phrases with question tags.

a *Twenty Thousand Leagues Under the Sea* was

written by Jules Verne, _____ ?

b The story is told by one of the passengers,

_____ ?

c The expedition sets sail from Long Island,

_____ ?

d The three protagonists are thrown overboard,

_____ ?

e The narrator had no idea how they survived the

storm, _____ ?

f Nobody knows what happened to the *Nautilus*,

_____ ?

C Reading

1 Look at the list of creatures.

> crocodile   duck   trout   elephant
> giraffe   python   poodle   dog
> rhinoceros   bull   salmon
> hippopotamus   shark   leopard

Quickly read the text on page 33. As you read, fill in the table, putting the names of the animals in the correct language column. Can any animals appear in more than one column?

English	Arabic	Greek	German	Latin

Name game: Where do animals get their names?

How did the hippo get such an odd name? Ever wondered who called Africa's largest leaf-eater a giraffe? We assume that many of these names have African roots, but this is not the case. Animals got their names from many different places and from many different languages.

Ducks, for example, are birds who 'duck' in the water. Their name comes from an old English word *duce*, which means a 'diver'.

The Arabic word *zirafoh*, which means 'long neck', gave the long-necked giraffe its name.

Two Greek words, *hippos*, which means 'horse', and *potamus*, which means 'river', were put together to give us the 'river horse' we know today as the hippopotamus.

The rhinoceros also got its name from two Greek words, *tinos*, which means 'nose', and *keras*, which means 'horn'. And 'horn on the nose' is a good description of this animal, which has just that – a horn on its nose.

Poodle dogs got their names from the German word *pudel*, which was short for *pudelhund*, which means 'a dog that splashes in water'.

The ancient Latin word *leopardus*, which means 'spotted lion', gave the leopard its name.

Bulls get their name from the old English word *belan*, which means to 'roar' or 'bellow'.

Both the Latin word *carcharus* and the Greek word *karckarios* mean 'sharp teeth', and it is from these two words that we get the name of the feared shark.

The salmon, which is known for its ability to leap out of the water as it swims upstream, also has a name of Latin origin. *Salmo*, in Latin, means 'leaping fish'.

Any fisherman will vouch for the fact that the trout is an avid eater and will go after any bait that moves. This greedy fish got its name from the Latin *trocta*, which means just that – 'greedy fish'.

The elephant gets its name from the ancient Greek *elephas* and the Latin *elephantus*. In Old English, the word was *oliphaunt*.

The Greek god Apollo killed a huge snake near Delphi, in Greece. Our modern-day 'python' comes from the Greek *puthon*.

Another two-word animal is the crocodile, and once again the name is made from two Greek words which describe its appearance: *kroke*, meaning 'small stone', and *drilos*, meaning 'worm'. So the meaning is 'worm of small stones'. At one time, in medieval English, the word was *cocodrille* and also *cokadrille*.

Adapted from 'Saving the wild orang-utan' by Reino Gevers, *Times of Oman*.

2   Read the text again, then decide which names describe the animal's behaviour and which describe its appearance. Which names do neither? Fill in the table.

Behaviour	Appearance	Neither

D Reading and writing

1 **Read the first paragraph of the newspaper article *Animals and birds can predict the weather*. It says that the weather affects:**

- the type of work we do
- what we wear
- what we eat
- the type of home we live in.

For each of the above, write two examples of how the weather affects your lifestyle.

Example: *The type of work we do: when it's very hot, we try not to work outside in the middle of the day.*

a The type of work we do

_____

_____

b What we wear

_____

_____

c What we eat

_____

_____

d The type of home we live in

_____

_____

Animals and birds can predict the weather

[1] Since the beginning of human times, we have looked to the weather on a daily basis. Weather has played a major role in the way we live our lives, the type of work we do, what we wear, what we eat and the types of homes we live in.

[2] For as long as humans have existed, people have tried to predict and forecast the weather. In early times, it was viewed as an essential factor for survival because knowing what the weeks and days ahead had in store enabled people to plant their crops, harvest, move location or the like. Forewarned is forearmed.

[3] Regular observations of the sun, moon and stars, and noting animal, bird and insect behaviour were the only facts that people were able to draw upon. Today, meteorologists use computers to forecast the weather, but 100% accuracy is still difficult, as the weather is influenced by factors such as warming of the oceans, the planets, and so on. Animals, birds, insects and plant life have a far greater ability to sense and interpret weather changes and signs than humans, and this is linked to their natural survival instincts.

Adapted from http://treechange.hubpages.com

2 **Imagine that the newspaper article is based on information obtained during an interview with a weather expert. What questions do you think the interviewer asked and what answers did the expert give? Write the interview. Start like this:**

Interviewer: *For how long have we looked at the weather?*

Expert: *Humans have looked at the weather on a daily basis since the beginning of human times.*

Int: *Why?*

Exp: *Because the weather has …*

_____

_____

_____

_____

_____

_____

_____

_____

_____

_____

_____

_____

_____

_____

_____

Unit 7: Can penguins see under water?

A Vocabulary

1 Use the code to find the five human senses and the parts of the body that use them.

1	2	3	4	5	6	7	8	9	10	11	12	13	14	15	16	17	18	19	20	21	22	23	24	25	26
a	b	c	d	e	f	g	h	i	j	k	l	m	n	o	p	q	r	s	t	u	v	w	x	y	z

a 19 9 7 8 20 / 5 25 5 19

_____

b 20 15 21 3 8 / 8 1 14 4 19

_____

c 20 1 19 20 5 / 20 15 14 7 21 5

_____

d 19 13 5 12 12 / 14 15 19 5

_____

e 8 5 1 18 9 14 7 / 5 1 18 19

_____

2 Perpetua is telling you her favourite object for each of her senses. Rewrite the sentences in full.

a For my (19 9 7 8 20) my (5 25 5 19) love to see a beautiful clear (19 11 25).

_____

b My (8 1 14 4 19) love to (20 15 21 3 8) the soft shiny fur of a (3 1 20).

_____

c My (20 15 14 7 21 5) loves to (20 1 19 20 5) fresh, juicy (6 18 21 9 20).

_____

d My (14 15 19 5) loves to (19 13 5 12 12) (7 18 1 19 19) that has just been cut.

_____

e My (5 1 18 19) love to (12 9 19 20 5 14) to the (19 15 14 7 19) that birds sing.

_____

35

3 Write **five** sentences to explain what you enjoy experiencing with your five senses.

a _____

b _____

c _____

d _____

e _____

4 Unjumble the letters to find the living creatures. Write them in your notebook.

Example: *gpnnuie = penguin*

> rfgadoynl   geael   acmnoelhe   sjlflheyi
> nta   ylf   futbytrle   umsoe   baibtr

5 Match each creature from Activity A4 to its description below.

Example: *It loves to swim in water and can keep its eyes open. = penguin*

a They have very complex eyes made of many different parts. _____

b Their wings can feel differences in the atmosphere. _____

c They use their feet to taste things. _____

d It might be watching you, even if it's got its back to you! _____

e A very sensitive insect that can feel vibrations in the ground. _____

f It can taste almost anything – and much more than you. _____

g It can see very far because of the shape of its eyes. _____

h It has eyes all over the place – why does it need so many?! _____

i If there is a sound, it can hear it! _____

B **Language focus: Comparative adverbs, -*ing* forms as subjects and after prepositions**

Comparative adverbs

1 Rearrange the words to make complete sentences.

a much better / than humans / dragonflies / do / see

_____

b than people / are able / bats / more clearly / to see / can

_____

c than animals / move faster / many fish / on land / water / through

_____

d other animals / more independently / chameleons / than / their eyes / can move

_____

e than humans / insects / more easily / things / do / sense

_____

f do / more / than birds / butterflies / efficiently / their wings / use

_____

2 Write **five** sentences about your country or family, using a comparative adverb in each one.

a _____

b _____

c _____

d _____

e _____

-ing forms as subjects and after prepositions

3 Complete the description by putting a suitable word in each gap.

> The -ing form of a verb can be used as a **(a)** _____ . It is common
> after certain **(b)** _____ , while other verbs are followed
> by the **(c)** _____ form; some verbs can be followed by either
> **(d)** _____ or an infinitive. Sometimes a **(e)** _____ can
> be the **(f)** _____ of a sentence or the **(g)** _____ of a
> preposition. Notice that when **(h)** _____ is followed by an -ing form,
> it tells us **(i)** _____ something is done.

C Reading

1 Read Part A of the text opposite, then complete the table. Give the name for each layer of the brain and explain what its functions are.

The brain

Part A

We take in information about the world through our five senses, which give us the ability to hear, smell, touch, see and taste. It is important that we learn to appreciate which of our senses we rely on most for our learning and learn to use them efficiently. It is also very important to train ourselves to use all our senses in our learning, so we can become better learners. On average, we only use 1–4% of our brain's potential. This means we have a lot of potential that we could use, but don't.

There are three layers to the brain. The top layer, the neocortex, is the thinking part, which is split into two parts, the right and left hemispheres. This layer deals with our creativity and logic. This is the biggest part of the human brain. The middle layer, known as the limbic layer, is the part that controls our emotions. It deals with our sense of identity and beliefs, and with our long-term memory. 'Reptilian' is the name for the lower layer. This is the survival part, which controls all the body's functions and instincts.

Adapted from www.sqa.org.uk

37

	Name	Function
top layer		
middle layer		
bottom layer		

2 Read Part B of the text, on page 38. Find words or phrases in the text that have a similar meaning to the following.

a features _____

b part or side _____

c sensible _____

d involving original or imaginative ideas _____

e producing a positive result _____

Part B

The top layer comprises 80% of the whole brain. It is involved in:

- thinking and problem solving
- speaking and language development
- reasoning and creative thought
- behaviour.

The left and right hemispheres have different characteristics, with the left hemisphere being associated with logical processes and the right hemisphere being associated with creative processes. We all use both sides of the brain to a greater or lesser degree, but most people have a natural preference for one hemisphere over the other. In other words, we are likely to respond in either a logical or a creative way to different learning experiences. Really effective thinking and learning uses both sides of the brain. If you know which side you prefer, you can learn to use your brain more effectively.

Adapted from www.sqa.org.uk

D Reading and writing

1 Read the article below, about animals and humans in sport and find out the following.

a Which animals are mentioned? _____

b Which sports people are mentioned? _____

c Which animal is the fastest? _____

d Which person is the fastest? _____

e Which animal is the strongest? _____

f Which person is the strongest? _____

Usain Bolt vs. the Cheetah: Olympians of the animal kingdom

The Summer Olympic Games sees many athletes vying for gold. But how would record-breaking runners, such as the fastest man in the world, Usain Bolt, fare against the wilder side of the animal kingdom?

Turns out, Usain Bolt would be left behind if he were to take certain four-leggers up on a challenge.

Animal athleticism would put to shame many a human Olympian, while humans would take home gold in athletic versatility.

Here's a look at some possible line-ups if some animals were to participate in the Olympic Games:

- Bolt ran 100 metres in 9.58 seconds, compared with the 5.8 seconds it would take a cheetah to cover that same distance.
- Kenyan runner David Rushida, world-record holder for the 800 metres, ran that distance in 1 minute 41 seconds. That's compared with a 33-second time for the pronghorn antelope and 49.2 seconds for a greyhound.
- World champ Mike Powell is known for his record-breaking jumps, reaching 8.95 metres in the long jump, but that's nothing for a red kangaroo, which can leap 12.8 metres.
- The animal kingdom also has a strong contender for the high jump: the snakehead fish can leap 4 metres out of the water, easily snatching the medal from athlete Javier Sotomayor, who jumps to 2.45 metres.
- Even Olympic weightlifters would have to contend with some fierce competition from the African elephant, which can lift 300 kilograms with its trunk and carry 820 kilograms, the grizzly bear, which can lift some 455 kilograms and the gorilla, which can lift a whopping 900 kilograms.

Adapted from www.livescience.com

2   Complete the table with information from the passage.

Sport	Olympian	Achievement	Animal	Achievement
Running	Usain Bolt	100 metres in 9.58 seconds	cheetah	5.8 seconds
	(a)	(b)	pronghorn antelope	(c)
Jumping	Mike Powell	(d)	(e)	(f)
	(g)	high jump 2.45 metres	(h)	(i)
Weightlifting			African elephant	lift 300 kg carry 820 kg
			(j)	(k)
			(l)	(m)

3   Find out who the fastest human swimmers are and which living creatures are the fastest in water. Then find out which human has flown the fastest and which creatures fly the fastest. Prepare a table similar to the one in Activity D2, then write a paragraph describing the achievements of humans and living creatures in the water and in the air.

_____

_____

_____

_____

_____

_____

_____

_____

_____

_____

_____

_____

_____

_____

_____

_____

_____

_____

Unit 8: How hot are chilli peppers?

A Vocabulary

1 Complete the crossword puzzle.

Clues

Across

2 Can be eaten (6)

3 Belonging to a place (10)

4 The opposite of spicy hot (4)

7 Improves (6)

10 Stop something unpleasant (7)

11 Cause (7)

13 Perspiration (liquid on skin) (5)

Down

1 Grown (10)

5 Full of (6)

6 Strong, effective (6)

8 Energy units (8)

9 As small as possible (7)

12 In the house (7)

2 **Use the answers from the crossword puzzle to complete these sentences.**

a Many plants and flowers grown in the garden are _____ .

b Some plants only thrive _____ and would not survive if they were put outside.

c The amount of meat that he eats is _____ because he prefers vegetables.

d He often takes something to _____ him of his headaches.

e She's always counting the number of _____ she eats.

f They say that _____ is 'tears from our skin'.

g He loves to eat curry, but only if it is _____ .

h Because of the climate, many different kinds of apples are _____ in the UK.

i The kangaroo is _____ to Australia. It cannot be found anywhere else.

j The sleeping draught he drank was very _____ and he fell asleep immediately.

k Coffee and cheese have been known to _____ headaches in many people.

l The cake was _____ with sugar and she found it much too sweet.

m Drinking lots of water _____ the quality of your skin.

3 Imagine you are describing the appearance of someone you know well (a family member, or a close friend). Which of the following words would you use? Which wouldn't you use?

> beanpole   beanstalk   ~~bony~~   delicate   featherweight
> fragile   lean   lightweight   pole   skeletal   skinny
> slight   slim   small   stick   undernourished   underweight

Positive connotation	Negative connotation
	bony

4 Look at the following descriptions and write in the missing apostrophes.

a He doesnt eat anything and looks undernourished.

b Shes got very delicate features and is the perfect shape for a dancer.

c Shes very fragile now and uses a walking stick to get about.

d The childrens skinny shape makes them look younger than they are.

e Shes quite small for her age, particularly compared to her sisters size.

f Hes as tall as a beanpole and wears his brothers clothes, which are too small for him.

B Language focus: Referring words and quantifiers

Referring words

1 Look back to pages 67–8 in your Coursebook and remind yourself about **referring words**. Then find the words below in the audioscript on page 153. What does each word or phrase refer back to? Complete the last column of the table.

Paragraph	Word/phrase	What it refers to
1	all of them	
2	our	
3	such plants	
4	The fruit	
5	them	

41

2 Fill in the gaps in the text below using suitable referring words.

Joachim and his sister used to live in the city and travel every day by train to school. It used to take **them** about an hour each way and **(a)** _____ used to arrive home feeling dirty and tired. Also, because **(b)** _____ mother worked in an office in the city, **(c)** _____ didn't get to see **(d)** _____ until late in the evening. By the time **(e)** _____ got home, it was very late and everybody was hungry, but **(f)** _____ wanted to cook. This meant **(g)** _____ had to buy fast food or something that was ready-made. Over time, **(h)** _____ diet affected **(i)** _____ health. **(j)** _____ decided to move to the countryside and bought a small house and went to a local school. In the countryside, **(k)** _____ lived a better life and ate a better diet!

3 For each referring word you added to the text above, say what it refers to.

Example: *them – Joachim and his sister*

a _____

b _____

c _____

d _____

e _____

f _____

g _____

h _____

i _____

j _____

k _____

Quantifiers

4 Fill the gaps in the sentences using a quantifier from the box. In some cases, more than one option is possible.

much	many
a lot of	most
a little	little
a few	few

a The teacher hasn't given us _____ essays to write this term.

b How _____ material are they expecting us to research for the project?

c Unfortunately, he's already had _____ problems with the new car.

d There are too _____ weeds in the garden.

e She didn't use _____ butter in her cake and that made a difference.

f   He's paid very _____ attention in the class.

g   It's only rained _____ times this year.

h   How much do _____ people do to help charities?

i   _____ of the advice the teacher gave has been helpful.

j   He only gave _____ help after promising so much.

k   He's great with computers and _____ people know as much as he does.

C Reading and writing

1   **Answer these questions about chilli peppers.**

   a   What do you know about the chilli pepper? Write down **at least three** things.

   _____

   _____

   _____

   b   How much does your family use chilli peppers?

   _____

   c   Can you think of any meals where chilli peppers are used? Write down **at least two**.

   _____

   _____

   d   Do you like chilli peppers? Why, or why not?

   _____

   e   What happens if you touch a chilli pepper and then touch your eyes? Has it ever happened to you?

   _____

2   **Look at the recipe on page 44. Complete the cooking instructions using the verbs in the box.**

   | add   cook   fry   serve   top |

2-bean chilli

About 500 g ground meat or vegetarian mince
1 large green pepper, chopped
1 large onion, chopped
2 tablespoons chilli powder
¼ teaspoon ground black pepper
2 x 400 g tin tomatoes
2 x 400 g tin beans (borlotti, kidney, etc.)
Sour cream/yoghurt

Cooking instructions

(a) _____ the mince, green peppers, onions, chilli powder and black pepper until the meat is brown. **(b)** _____ the tomato juice and beans and **(c)** _____ everything. **(d)** _____ with sour cream or yoghurt. **(e)** _____ with rice or naan bread.

3 Think about how you could change the recipe. What might you add or take away in your country? For example in Cyprus you might add herbs such as oregano.

a Would you use meat or not? If so, what would you use?

_____

b Would you use sour cream or yoghurt?

_____

c Would you serve it with naan bread or rice?

_____

d Which beans would you use?

_____

e Would you use tinned or fresh tomatoes?

_____

4 Write the new recipe and the cooking instructions, using your ideas from Activity C3.

_____
_____
_____
_____
_____
_____
_____
_____
_____
_____
_____
_____
_____

Unit 9: Who was Ibn Battuta?

A Vocabulary

1 **Complete the sentences using words and phrases from the box.**

came to an agreement
found   found his way
go up   shown
travel around
tried to get to
understood
went by boat

a I _____ that he said we should 'call' him not 'visit' him.

b He slowly _____ through the crowds of people to reach his destination.

c She loves to _____ when she goes to different countries; she's not the sort of person who just sits on a beach.

d He _____ all along the coast rather than travel by train.

e They were _____ the pyramids and given a good history lesson.

f Because of the bad weather, it took them two days to _____ the mountain.

g They finally _____ the site they had spent many years looking for.

h She _____ the top of the mountain, but had no energy left.

i They finally _____ on how much they should pay.

2 **Use these words and phrases to make up your own complete and correct sentences. Use two or more words and phrases in a sentence if you want. Try to write five sentences.**

but make no mistake   capacity   copious   in an era   pilgrimage
primary   proficient in   prose   scribe   thereby   transcribing
wise beyond his years   zigzagging

_____

_____

_____

_____

_____

B Language focus: Countries, nationalities and languages, past perfect tense

1 Add other countries, nationalities and languages to the lists below. Use the information on page 76 of your Coursebook to help you.

Countries that end in -*land* and -*a*	Nationalities that end in -*ese* and -*ian*	Languages that end in -*ian* and -*n*
Greenland	Taiwanese	Italian
India	Indian	Russian

Past perfect tense

2 Look at this example situation: You left your new pet puppy on its own for the first time. When you got home, what did you find?

- It had eaten my shoes.
- It had torn all the toilet paper and left it all over the floor.
- It had spilled all its water.
- It had destroyed the carpet.

For each situation below, think of two or three things that you found when you got home.

a You forgot to turn off the tap in the kitchen sink.

_____

_____

_____

b Your sister was playing alone in your bedroom.

_____

_____

_____

c A wild animal got into your house.

_____

_____

_____

d Your mother had been ill and arrived home from hospital.

_____

_____

_____

C Reading

1 You are going to read a text about space travel. Here are the six paragraph headings:

A *Even faster*

B *Inter-planet transport*

C *Spaceships with sails*

D *Today's technology*

E *Warp speed*

F *Wind power*

In which paragraph do you think you will find the following words and phrases? Use a dictionary to check anything you are unsure about.

a new world ☐

better technologies ☐

15th and 16th centuries ☐

one planet to another ☐

rowing ☐

science-fiction authors ☐

scientists dream ☐

several years younger ☐

solar winds ☐

steam engines ☐

the earth's winds ☐

time slows down ☐

2 **Skim the text below. Decide which heading matches each paragraph and write the heading in the gap.**

3 **Look at the text again and find the words and phrases from Activity C1. Were you correct about the paragraphs?**

4 **What do these words and phrases mean?**

a enormous (paragraph 1) _____

b current (2) _____

c ancestors (2) _____

d immense (2) _____

e solar (3) _____

f whisk (3) _____

g descendants (4) _____

h marvel (4) _____

i authors (5) _____

j debate (5) _____

Spaceship or sailing boat?

(1) _____
The great explorers who came to the new world in the 15th and 16th centuries came on enormous sailing boats. They could have rowed, but that would have taken too long. Steam engines had not yet been invented, nor would they be invented for a long time, but this did not stop people. Rather than wait around for better things to be invented, they used the powerful winds to carry them across the large unknown waters.

(2) _____
Today, we could set out on a long, slow journey across the galaxy, but with current technology it would take us much too long to get anywhere, very much like the ancient explorers trying to reach the new world by rowing. We could wait around possibly for centuries for better technologies, such as a warp-drive device. Or we can do as our ancestors did – use the power of the wind to carry us across the immense space between us and the stars.

(3) _____
Engineers and scientists are currently exploring the possibility of creating spaceships with large, wing-like sails. In the same way that the sails of a sailing boat catch the earth's winds, the sails of these spacecraft would catch the solar winds of the sun and whisk them to other stars. The larger the sail, the faster the craft would be able to travel and, if large enough, it would be able to reach amazing speeds, perhaps even the speed of light – 300,000 kilometres per second.

(4) _____
Just as we study Christopher Columbus's 'discovery' of America using the limited technology of the times, it is

likely that, 500 years from now, our descendants will look at us and marvel at the discovery of a new world. And, just as now we can travel from the East to the West in a matter of hours, perhaps in the future we will have technology that will allow people to be transported from one planet to another in a matter of hours.

(5) _____
Warp speed has been the subject of science and science fiction for many years. Scientists dream of technologies that will allow us to travel through the many galaxies faster than the speed of light. Science-fiction authors use these dreams to create wonderfully entertaining stories. In order to qualify as warp speed, a craft must be able to travel at speeds faster than the speed of light. There is a lot of debate as to whether or not this is even possible. Many scientists say that the speed of light is the absolute fastest possible rate of travel. Others say that just because we have not found a way to travel faster than the speed of light, it does not mean it is not possible.

(6) _____
If science is able to create a way of travelling faster than the speed of light, there are many interesting and strange effects. These effects include the possibility that time slows down for space travellers. This means that, while on a journey, they may age at a slower rate than everyone back on Earth. As a result, when they return, they might be several years younger than people who were the same age as them when they left. Perhaps you will be the one to discover this type of technology.

Adapted from www.kidsastronomy.com

D Reading and writing

1 **What do you think *caving* is? Tick one of the options below.**

a   It is the exploration of cave systems. ☐

b   It is using a place underground to store food. ☐

c   It is an activity where deep holes are dug to find things. ☐

Quickly read the following text to check your answer.

> Exploration of *caves* takes us into a world much different from that above ground – a world of darkness surrounded by rock and mud. Exotic *formations*, streams and waterfalls, tight *crawlways*, deep *canyons* and pits, huge rooms with large blocks of breakdown, *crickets*, bats and cave rats await the cave explorer.
>
> Caving can be a *strenuous* sport, a casual hobby, a means to conducting scientific research or all of these and more. Caves are found around the world and in a variety of settings, from cold alpine environments to warm tropical rain forests, and are formed through a variety of natural processes.
>
> Adapted from cavingintro.net

2 **Match the words in italics in the text with the definitions below.**

a   A type of flying insect. _____

b   A passageway where you move forward on your hands and knees, or with your body close to the ground. _____

c   A large natural hollow in the side of a hill or cliff, or underground. _____

d   Something that has been made.

_____

e   A narrow valley between hills or mountains.

_____

f   Using a lot of energy. _____

3 **Imagine your class wants to go caving. Do the following:**

■   Choose a destination (you will need to research this).

■   Make a list of the clothes, food, navigation and communication equipment you should take.

■   Make a list of ten top tips for the trip, for example: *Check the weather forecast before you go, as it can be very dangerous if heavy rain is forecast.*

_____

_____

_____

_____

_____

_____

_____

_____

_____

_____

_____

_____

_____

_____

_____

_____

_____

When you have all the information, design a leaflet for the students in your class to give to their parents and friends.

Unit 10: What's the best job for a teenager?

A Vocabulary

1 How many jobs can you remember from Unit 10 of the Coursebook? Match the job to the description in the table.

bike courier	works in a safari park to stop monkeys escaping
cat food quality controller	delivers packages around a city
hippotherapist	arranges furniture for the best flow of energy
ethical hacker	stands without moving for hours
Brazilian mosquito researcher	smells and feels animal food
monkey chaser	uses horses to help people with disabilities
Buckingham Palace guard	tries to find treatments for malaria
Feng Shui consultant	makes sure companies' software is secure

2 Look at the following words. Decide if each word is an adjective or a noun, then choose **one** noun and **one** adjective to complete the sentences below.

constant	substantial	proficiency
brutal	timber	shortages
criteria	desirable	likelihood
~~stretches~~	severe	~~hostile~~

Example: *Hostile stretches of desert continue for many kilometres, and many have failed to complete the trek.*

a _____ _____ of milk prevented many dairy products from being produced.

b The _____ of _____ violence hindered the TV crew from covering the story fully.

c There is a _____ supply of renewable _____ from Norway.

d There are _____ _____ on which to base your job application.

e It is _____ to have a good _____ in English for the job.

B Language focus: Direct speech and reported statements, sentence adverbs

Direct speech and reported statements

1 Change the sentences on page 50 into reported speech using the prompts.

Example: '*I can't come tomorrow, so please cancel the class.*'
He said that he couldn't come the next day and to cancel the class.

49

a 'Come to the cinema with me tonight.'

He invited _____

_____ .

b 'I'll bring back your book tomorrow.'

He promised _____

_____ .

c 'Don't be late again or you'll lose your job.'

He warned _____

_____ .

d 'You took my bag. I saw you!'

She accused _____

_____ .

e 'He always asks the same student to give the answers.'

They complained _____

_____ .

f 'I think you should try this restaurant as the food is excellent.'

He recommended _____

_____ .

g 'I didn't steal your bag. I wasn't in the room.'

He denied _____

_____ .

h 'Why don't you take the bus instead of driving?'

He suggested _____

_____ .

2 **Read the job interview opposite, then report what was said.**

A: Good morning. Now, let me check something. Have you applied for the job of travel representative?

B: Good morning. Yes. And I specifically asked to be based in Greece because I speak fluent Greek.

A: Have you ever been to Greece and specifically the Peloponnisos area?

B: I've been to Greece, yes, but I don't know that area very well. I'm more familiar with northern Greece.

A: That shouldn't be a problem. What would you say was one of the biggest issues with this job?

B: Well, the hours are quite long and not very regular.

A: Would you be available to work overtime?

B: Yes, of course.

A: Could you tell me what you think of the salary? Is it reasonable?

B: Yes, it's fine and I know I will earn commission too.

A: Good. Now let's look at …

_____

_____

_____

_____

_____

_____

_____

_____

_____

_____

_____

_____

_____

_____

_____

Sentence adverbs

3 Use the correct sentence adverb to complete the sentences.

> Exactly   Definitely   Sadly   Certainly
> Absolutely   Obviously   Unsurprisingly
> Luckily   Probably

a _____ he won't be with us next year, as he's moved onto a different job.

b _____ they won't be coming with us, as they're not here yet.

c _____ they have no interest in the music, as it's from a different generation.

d _____ I went to the shop early and they hadn't sold out of milk.

e _____ ! That's what I asked you to do because I knew how he would react.

f _____ count me in. I would love to come with you.

g _____ , no he won't make it, as he's already running late.

h _____ ! We'd love to help at the charity event.

i _____ yes! He would be an excellent asset to the team, so include him.

C Reading

1 You are going to read about the two jobs: **A pilot** and **B actor**. In which text do you think you will see the following words and phrases? Write A or B next to each one. Use reference sources to check anything you are not sure about.

a 750 hours of structured learning
b air guitar
c airline

d aviation law
e blockbuster
f equipment
g fashion shoots
h Hollywood
i intensive training
j programme
k lot of standing around
l meteorology
m Royal Air Force
n superstardom
o world tour

2 Match the words and phrases in column A from the texts with an appropriate meaning from column B.

A	B
average	best-seller
blockbuster	follow
brush up	get
consistently	jobs
intensive	needing a lot of effort
obtain	normal, usual
occupations	regularly
undergo	revise, practise

3 Read the text below and on the next page, then check your answers to Activities C1 and C2.

A Pilot

Being a pilot – whether for an airline or as a fighter pilot – has consistently remained in the top five most glamorous occupations since the 1940s.

Reality check: You'll need to be prepared for an intensive training programme. To obtain your commercial pilot's licence (CPL), you'll have to undergo a minimum 750 hours of structured learning on all aspects of flying, including meteorology and aviation law, followed by 150 hours of flight training over a 14-month period.

Typical salary: £24,000 as a newly qualified pilot in the Royal Air Force, rising to £60,000 as captain; and £73,792 to £100,000 for an airline pilot.

51

B Actor

You could be starring in the latest blockbuster, enjoying the red carpet that Hollywood superstardom brings. Or you might prefer to do 'proper' acting work in a theatre.

Reality check: The average actor is out of work 90% of the time, so make sure you brush up on your other skills.

Typical salary: You can get £80 a day for extra work, whilst a Hollywood superstar can bring in anything up to £20 million a movie.

4 Read the text again and answer these questions.

a For how long has the job of pilot been glamorous?

_____

b How many hours of structured learning and flight training does someone need to complete?

_____

c Name **two** subjects that trainee pilots will study.

_____

d Which **two** types of acting work are mentioned?

_____

e Why should actors practise their other skills?

_____

D Reading and writing

1 Read these newspaper adverts for summer jobs. Which job would you like to apply for? Why? Write about 80 words, giving your choice and your reasons.

Need to earn some summer cash?

Come and work in our International Students' Coffee Shop!
€6–8 per hour with tips and meals provided
Good spoken English is required
Training provided
Contact: Michael Stooge (CoffeeShop@everymail.com)

Students needed!

Library/administrative work
20 hours a week – June and July
Good knowledge of English and computers necessary
Suitable for someone who likes a quiet environment
Contact: Jane Phelps (jphelps@unicity.org)

_____

_____

_____

_____

_____

_____

_____

_____

_____

2 Read this email from a student, applying for the job at the International Students' Coffee Shop. What is wrong with it? Cross out and correct the mistakes.

Hi Michael

I want to apply for the job in the newspaper for the coffee shop. I've not worked in a coffee shop before but that don't matter as you give training. I've got good English because I have been going to special English classes at the university. I love talking to people and so lots of customers would come if I worked their. The money is fine and so hope to hear from you soon.

Love Michelle

3 In your notebook, write your own email, applying for the library/administrative job.

Unit 11: Who are the Maasai?

A Vocabulary

1 Use a word or phrase from each of the six columns to write **seven** complete sentences. There are many possible sentences.

Sports	~~sportswear~~	reach	~~always~~	shaped	35 metres.
Men	shoes	in how	to	more than	feet.
~~The correct~~	throwers	~~is~~	distances of	African	of football.
The Maasai	flexibility	have	different	manufactured	hyphens.
Swamp football	are	are	often	use	worldwide.
There is	and women	unusual	indigenous	the game	~~important.~~
Some tuna	is an	an	form of	~~very~~	group.

Example: *The correct sportswear is always very important.*

1 _____

2 _____

3 _____

4 _____

5 _____

6 _____

7 _____

2 Join each word in column A with a word in column B to make compound words about sports.

A	B
underwater	jumping
bungee	running
tuna	diving
apple	jumping
land	rugby
marathon	race
swamp	pulling
potato	football
canoe	wrestling
indoor	throwing
goat	kite-flying

3 **Which sport from Activity A2 is being described in each of these sentences?**

a In this sport, you jump from a great height and then bounce up again! _____

b This is a long-distance race, often run in cities and towns. _____

c In this sport, you end up very dirty, unlike the game we see on TV every weekend. _____

d Pushing against water and holding your breath for a long time are very important. _____

e There is no wasted food in this sport. _____

f The poor animal does not enjoy this sport, which is played by men on horses. _____

g To love water and to understand the sea are very important in this sport. _____

h A very dangerous sport! You throw yourself from a great height and your head must hit the ground! _____

i Children, as well as adults, enjoy this sport. Balance and focus are very important. _____

j You need lots of strength for this sport, as the fish can weigh many kilos. _____

k You need a large empty space for this sport and a very light object. _____

4 **What do the words below have in common? Separate them equally into the four columns.**

warrior	tendons
Maasai	shoe
Tanzania	runner
Sahara	footwear
bones	credit card
ligaments	iPads
Athens	Kenya
muscles	soldier

Column A	Column B	Column C	Column D
tendons			

Column A describes _____

Column B describes _____

Column C describes _____

Column D describes _____

B Language focus: Word building, -ing forms

Word building

1   Fill in the table. You may not be able to write something in all the gaps.

Verb	Noun	Adjective	Adverb
		common	
absorb			
provide			
	entirety		
			excessively
stabilise			
	severity		
encourage			

2   Use **eight** different words from Activity B1 to write sentences of your own.

_____

_____

_____

_____

_____

_____

_____

_____

_____

-ing forms

3   Choose the correct word from the box to complete the sentences. You will need to change the word into its -ing form.

spend	drive	sing
wait	carry	lie
teach	play	
paint	chew	

a   She loved the concert. The _____ was excellent.

b   That's her favourite lesson. The _____ is always very good.

c   Please throw your gum away. _____ in class is so rude.

d   He's the best modern artist. His _____ is so colourful.

e   Young people don't have much money. Their _____ is very limited.

f   _____ at night can be quite stressful.

g   Don't believe what she says. Her _____ is constant nowadays.

h   _____ with my friends is my favourite pastime.

i   _____ for them at the restaurant was not a good idea.

j   She walked into the room _____ a heavy bag.

C Reading

1 You are going to read about the world's ten most dangerous sports.

BASE jumping	rock fishing
bike riding	solo yacht racing
bull riding	speed skiing
cave diving	street luging
free diving	supercross

What do you think each sport involves? Use a paper or digital reference source to check any words you are unsure about.

2 These 20 words and phrases are taken from the text you are going to read. Which sport do you think each refers to? Use a paper or digital reference source to check any words you are unsure about.

120 metres under water   _____

aerodynamic suits   _____

broken bones   _____

can still be dangerous   _____

cave creature   _____

divers are well trained   _____

fly in the air   _____

handlebars   _____

highly modified skateboards   _____

incredibly dangerous sport   _____

it's not exactly legal   _____

massive waves   _____

non-motorised sport   _____

not getting enough oxygen   _____

pavement   _____

pirates   _____

sharks   _____

tides   _____

try to hang on   _____

very dangerous   _____

3 Skim the text below and decide which sport from Activity C1 belongs in each gap. Write them in.

The world's most dangerous sports

(a) _____

BASE stands for Building, Antenna, Span and Earth. These are the fixed objects that experts in this incredibly dangerous sport jump from. BASE jumpers will jump with a parachute off any tall structure, including skyscrapers, electrical towers, bridges and cliffs. In the past, BASE jumpers have leapt from the Golden Gate Bridge, the Eiffel Tower and the Empire State Building. People who try this sport almost always end up arrested (it's not exactly legal) and some don't even live long enough to get arrested (we told you it was dangerous).

(b) _____

Divers will plunge up to 120 metres under water in a single breath. At the 2001 Free Diving World Cup, 15 people had to be rescued because of blackouts caused by their brains not getting enough oxygen.

(c) _____

Imagine being more than 30 metres under water in a deep, cold and dark cave. Divers are well trained, but there are so many things that can go wrong, which is why this is one of the world's most dangerous sports. You can lose your way, or run out of air; your equipment can fail, or you can be eaten alive by a cave creature.

(d) _____

This is the world's fastest non-motorised sport and one of the world's most dangerous sports. Skiers wear special skis and aerodynamic suits to fly down a hill at speeds up to 250 kilometres per hour! That's almost as fast as a racing car! One crash often means death.

(e) _____

Unless you're a fish, how can fishing be one of the world's most dangerous sports? The sport involves casting a line into the ocean from the shoreline. People often forget about the tides and are swept away, or are dragged underwater by massive waves. In 2001, 15 people in Australia died while doing this sport.

(f) _____

Jump on a raging bull that hates your guts and try to hang on. That's the name of the game in this sport. Some of the bulls weigh over 900 kilograms and can throw a rider off in a split second – and may even stomp on the rider afterwards. Riders suffer broken bones, punctured lungs and even death.

(g) _____

Athletes fly in the air on a motorcycle, while doing backflips, taking their hands off the handlebars, and other death-defying stunts.

(h) _____

In a race around the world, sailors encounter waves, sharks, hurricanes and even pirates. The nearest help can be hundreds of kilometres away and racers have no control over the conditions they run into. With no one nearby to help them out, racers can lose the race – and their lives.

(i) _____

Highly modified skateboards are used to race down a hill at speeds up to 130 kilometres per hour. The pioneers of this sport originally raced down hills in the middle of traffic, which made it even more risky. There are now special luges and equipment for the sport, which make it much safer. But hey, you're still hitting the pavement when you crash.

(j) _____

We've all heard the phrase 'it's as easy as riding a bike'. Well, riding a bike can still be very dangerous. In 2001, more kids broke bones or dislocated joints riding bicycles than any other sport.

Adapted from www.kidzworld.com

4   Look at the text again and check whether your predictions in Activity C2 were correct. Tick the ones you got right.

D   Reading and writing

1   You are going to read a blog from a parent who thinks that children should be allowed to take part in extreme sports. Before you read, what reasons do you think the parent might give? Try to think of **five**.

_____

_____

_____

_____

2   Read the blog and see if your reasons are the same or different.

Extreme sports for kids are great, because they really challenge them and make them believe and trust in themselves. It makes them more aware of what they can and can't do, and pushes them to do things that perhaps normally they wouldn't do. Forget the dangers, as that's part of the challenge and makes a child respect their body more. It also raises awareness of what the body can do. The kid who does extreme sports is the kid who stands out in a group; they're different and have confidence in themselves. They like to be different and go to places that most children probably just look at on their computers. The kid who does extreme sports is the kid who does it and doesn't just sit on the couch looking at it being done. Challenge your kid, get them out and doing things that will really get their adrenalin flowing and make them remember they're alive.

3   You are now going to write your own blog about children taking part in extreme sports. First of all, decide if you agree or disagree with the comments made in the blog above. If you agree, use your own blog to say why you agree and give more reasons for supporting the writer. If you disagree, give clear reasons.

_____

_____

_____

_____

_____

_____

_____

_____

_____

_____

_____

Unit 12: What does a triathlete do?

A Vocabulary

1 Look at the table on the right. Complete the information about football. Then think of two more sports and add information about these as well.

what / name?	football		
where / play?	on a pitch		
when / play?			
what / equipment?			
how many / players?			
aim / game?	to get the most goals		
how / win?			

2 Write **ten** questions and answers using information from the table above.

Example: *What is the name of the game?*
The name of the game is football.

_____

_____

_____

_____

_____

_____

_____

_____

_____

_____

3 Match the following words to make two- or three-word phrases. Some are noun + noun, some are verb + noun, some are adjective + noun. Then use the phrases to complete the sentences on page 59.

excellent	moisture	properly	time-keeper
fit	speed	better	thick
absorb	better	~~lenses~~	two-piece suits
body	ventilation	long-lasting	lightweight
fit	current	measured	~~contact~~

Example: *contact + lenses = contact lenses*
He uses contact lenses when he goes cycling because they're more comfortable than glasses.

a These days, you sweat less in sports clothes because they have better

   _____ and _____ .

b They now make _____ for women that are very comfortable.

c The sofa was covered in a _____ material.

d If they continue at their _____ , the time will be better than last
   year's record.

e If you are _____ , then the suit should be a _____ .

f 'If you'd learn to tell the time, then maybe you'd be a _____ !'

g The suit was an _____ and did not hang off him like the other
   style did.

B Language focus: Sentence patterns with comparatives, 'signpost' words, future forms

Sentence patterns with comparatives

1 Look at the information about two different running shoes. Using comparative structures, write **at least five** sentences comparing the two products.

	Go Fast Pro	Leisure Extra
Price	$129 (adults), $99 (children)	$59 (adults)
Sizes	sizes for adults and children, and different width sizes available	adults only, one width size
Colours	12 different colours	blue/black/white/red
Material	leather shoe, rubber sole	plastic shoe, rubber sole
Comfort	excellent all-round comfort and support, for long periods of sport	comfortable for short periods
Availability	all sports outlets, as well as online from www.gofastpro.sn	supermarkets only
Weight	280 grams	390 grams
Use	road and track	all-purpose

_____

_____

_____

_____

_____

2 Think of **two** more sports products (not running shoes). Find out information about them. Put the information into a table, then compare the two products.

'Signpost' words

3 **Fill in the gaps in the following sentences with an appropriate 'signpost' word.**

a You can buy quite cheap wetsuits these days,

_____ the problem is that they tend

to be made of thick material which is not very

flexible. _____ , this makes body

movement quite difficult.

b Goggles are really important, _____

the shape and how much you spend is up to you.

c _____ , these may be a good option

for swimmers who use contact lenses.

d _____ , they are more aerodynamic

_____ offer better ventilation for

the wearer.

e _____ , if your feet are soft and

susceptible to blisters, you should invest in a

good pair of socks that can absorb moisture

properly.

Future forms

4 **Complete the sentences using the correct future form from the box.**

| will going to will be seeing leaves |
| is meeting going to will |

a When is he _____ compete in the next

race?

b Lie down quietly and rest: that _____

help your headache.

c The nominations for the next Olympic Games

are _____ be announced soon.

d He _____ some friends after work.

e The train only _____ when all the

seats are full.

f They _____ carry your bag if it is

too heavy.

g I _____ the headteacher later today.

C Reading

1 **You are going to read about an adventure holiday in Costa Rica, where you can do some unusual sporting activities. Which of the following words and phrases do you think will appear in the text you are going to read? Use paper or digital reference sources to check any words you are unsure of.**

beach volleyball	☐	palm trees	☐
bird watching	☐	rainforest	☐
cave diving	☐	scenic boat trip	☐
desert	☐	tigers	☐
fireworks display	☐	tropical nature	☐
hanging bridges	☐	volcano	☐
horse riding	☐	waterfalls	☐
mountains	☐	whale watching	☐

2 **Match each word in column A with an appropriate meaning from column B.**

A	B
lodge	brave
canals	paths or tracks
trails	small building, often in a forest or jungle
daring	waterways

3 **Look at these phrases from the text. What do they mean?**

a banana plantations

_____

b bird's eye view

_____

c fireworks display

_____

d hot springs

_____

e interactive exhibits

_____

f narrow waterways

_____

g rafting trip

_____

4 Skim the text and check which of the words and phrases from Activity C1 appear.

Costa Rica discovery

Rainforest, mountains and both Caribbean and Pacific coasts make Costa Rica the perfect place to explore tropical nature.

Day 1: After a quick tour of San José, we will visit the National Museum and stop at the INBio Park. This is a wonderful educational and recreational centre, where the numerous **(a)** _____ will provide your family with a fascinating introduction to Costa Rica.

Day 2: The next morning, we make our way to the coastal Caribbean lowlands. We will take a scenic boat trip along the **(b)** _____ of Tortuguero National Park that will lead us to a hidden riverbank lodge in the rainforest. Here we can see toucans and many other brightly coloured birds in the trees, and perhaps crocodiles in the water, as we explore the natural and man-made canals.

Day 3: Travelling back down the river, we will continue the journey through **(c)** _____ , palm trees and papayas growing along the roadside until we reach Sarapiqui. Situated on the banks of the Puerto Viejo River and the nearby Braulio Carrillo National Park, Sarapiqui is one of the best areas for bird watching.

Day 4: Upon arrival, there will be time to relax, as well as the option to enjoy a **(d)** _____ , or horse riding in the forest for some fantastic fun. There is also the opportunity to visit the Rainforest Alliance Banana Project, where we can tour the eco-friendly project and learn about local environmental issues.

Day 5: Next we will visit Arenal Volcano; home to some wonderful natural **(e)** _____ , waterfalls and the impressively active Arenal Volcano. We will also explore the nearby forest trails and watch for a variety of birdlife near the volcano. On a clear night, you can swim in the thermal springs and safely watch the volcano spluttering lava into the night air like a wonderful **(f)** _____ .

Day 6: Continuing on to Monteverde, we will explore the National Park's trails – both above the trees and below! The included Sky Walk takes us across hanging bridges high above the forest for a **(g)** _____ . The more daring can choose to zipwire through the trees!

Day 7: Finally, there's time to relax on golden Pacific Ocean beaches in Manuel Antonio National Park, where capuchin monkeys play in the overhanging palm trees.

Adapted from GrandAmericanAdventures.com

5 Read the text again and fill the gaps with the phrases from Activity C3.

D Reading and writing

1 Here are some possible future sports. Put a tick (√) against those you think could happen and a cross (X) against those you think are unlikely.

Moon golf ☐

Race-car flying ☐

Space diving ☐

Lunar or Mars spelunking (pot holing) ☐

Climbing the eight summits (the highest mountain on each planet) ☐

Lunar dust skiing (on the moon) ☐

Hover boarding ☐

2 Choose **two** of the sports from Activity D1 and write a paragraph (60–80 words) about them in your own words. Look at this example paragraph.

Hover boarding

Hover boarding is a sport that first became popular after being shown in science-fiction films in the 1990s. The idea caught on and is now a popular pastime for many teenagers. The sport is played anywhere and any time the participants are free. All you need is your hover board and the boots that are attached to it. People either 'hover' by themselves or with friends. There is no real aim to the sport, apart from becoming skilful in the various moves. If someone participates in a competition, then the winner is the most skilful hover boarder.

_____

_____

_____

_____

_____

_____

_____

3 Use the words below to make questions about hover boarding. Then use the information in the paragraph to answer them.

a what / name?_____

_____

b where / play?_____

_____

c when / play?_____

_____

d what / equipment? _____

_____

e how many / players? _____

_____

f aim / game?_____

_____

g how / win? _____

_____

Unit 13: How much water do you use?

A Vocabulary

1 Choose a word or phrase from each column in the table to make six complete sentences (the seventh has been done as an example). Write them out in full.

The world	have	pulls	up	~~oxygen and~~	oceans
Scientists	~~is a~~	only about	about	of the earth's	chemicals
~~Water~~	are not	~~compound~~	they	of	languages
The Moon's	around us	from about	~~of~~	different	chemicals
Languages	has borrowed	is made	120	in the earth's	water
English	gravity	static	the water	120	dynamic
Humans	use	discovered	0.3%	are	~~hydrogen~~

Example: *Water is a compound of oxygen and hydrogen.*

_____

_____

_____

_____

_____

_____

2 Use the code to make words and phrases.

1	2	3	4	5	6	7	8	9	10	11	12	13	14	15	16	17	18	19	20	21	22	23	24	25	26
a	b	c	d	e	f	g	h	i	j	k	l	m	n	o	p	q	r	s	t	u	v	w	x	y	z

a 20 5 13 16 5 18 1 20 21 18 5

_____

b 16 15 15 18 / 8 25 7 9 5 14 5

_____

c 19 23 5 1 20

_____

d 23 1 20 5 18 / 22 1 16 15 21 18

_____

e 23 5 9 7 8 20

_____

f 6 18 5 5 26 5

_____

g 6 9 19 8 / 20 1 14 11

_____

h 6 18 21 9 20 / 1 14 4 / 22 5 7 5 20 1 2 12 5 19

_____

i 8 5 1 12 20 8 / 16 18 15 2 12 5 13 19

_____

j 19 9 14 11 19 / 1 14 4 / 20 15 9 12 5 20 19

_____

3 **Use the words and phrases from Activity A2 to complete these sentences.**

   a They have a very unhealthy diet and do not eat any _____ .

   b The _____ in the school need to be cleaned more often, as they are used by many children.

   c The world's _____ is rising and many places are experiencing water shortages.

   d You need to keep a check on your _____ and make sure it is stable.

   e Men tend to _____ much more than women when exercising.

   f They will _____ , as they did not take very many clothes with them.

g _____ is an area that should be taught more in school.

h Their _____ is full of some very exotic types now and they have spent a lot of money on it.

i _____ often results in rain, but not enough in some countries.

j _____ later in life can often be prevented if you respect your body when you are young.

4 **Look at these pairs of words. In each pair, one of the words is spelt incorrectly. Circle it.**

   a sceintist   chemicals
   b recognise   equivelent
   c billingual   dictionary
   d referance   sources
   e definitons   organism
   f properties   artifical
   g intreact   aluminium
   h discovered   attration
   i electronmagnets nucleus
   j equivelent   bilingual

5 **Put the corrected words in the grid below to find the name of a country that has serious water shortages.**

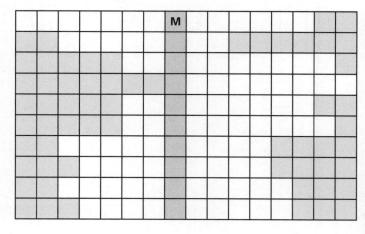

6 The words below are all new to the English language. Notice how many of them are connected with technology. Write the correct word next to the definitions. Can you think of any words to add to the list?

> app   e-ruitment   hoody   chillaxing
> audiophile   fashionista   netiquette
> couch potato   buzzword   freemale
> chatroom   cyber café

a Set of rules on how you should behave when you use the Internet. _____

b A person who spends a lot of time in front of the television. _____

c A person who likes and purchases a lot of audio material. _____

d When a person applies for a job via the Internet. _____

e A woman who is happy to remain single and independent. _____

f A new and fashionable word. _____

g Short for software application. _____

h A person who dresses according to the latest fashion trends. _____

i An item of clothing that young people often wear. _____

j A blend of 'chilling' and 'relaxing'. _____

k A place on the Internet where people communicate through typed messages. _____

l A place that provides internet access to the public. _____

B Language focus: The passive form, word building

The passive form

1 The passive voice is used when we want to focus attention on the person or thing affected by the action. Which of the following sentences are examples of the passive form?

a Two hundred people are employed by the car manufacturer in our town. ☐

b The headteacher invited all the children to the opening ceremony. ☐

c Running water was supplied to all villages by an international charity. ☐

2 Put the correct form of the passive verb in the following sentences, then complete them with the words in the box.

> **Verbs:** known   deliver   make (x2)   use (x2)
> cause   need   cover   mix
>
> **Words:** hydrogen   seawater   oil
> salt   fires   homes   dehydration
> irrigation   earth   water

a About 70% of Earth's surface _____ with _____ .

b Water _____ up of two elements: _____ and oxygen.

c Water _____ to people's _____ by the water industry.

d Ocean tides _____ by the rotation of the _____ .

e Water from the sea is _____ as _____ .

f Seawater _____ up of about 35 grams of dissolved _____ for every kilogram of seawater.

g _____ separates from water when it _____ together.

h Drinking water _____ by humans to avoid _____ .

i Water _____ in agricultural _____ to grow crops.

j Water _____ frequently by fire fighters to extinguish _____ .

Word building

3 Fill in the gaps in the table.

Verb	Noun	Adjective	Adverb
limit		limited	
	discovery	discoverable	discoverably
differ		different	
include	inclusion		
	combination	combinational	
exert	exertion	exertive	
depend		dependable	
	shortage		
power			powerfully

4 Fill the gaps in the sentences below using the correct word from the table in Activity B3.

a A _____ (noun) of water and salt make up the world's seawater.

b The _____ (adjective) supply of water in many countries is a serious future concern.

c The waterfall surged _____ (adverb), producing an amazing force of energy.

d To _____ (verb) water conservation in a biology lesson's curriculum is sensible.

e The villagers _____ (verb) very much on the one water supply in the village.

f The _____ (adjective) flavours in the food made it extremely tasty.

g Some areas of the world have huge _____ (noun), whereas others have an excess.

h The _____ (noun) of penicillin changed the face of medical development.

i She is very _____ (adjective) and looks after the home when her parents are away.

j 'If you _____ (verb) a bit more energy, you'll probably find it easier to open.'

C Reading

1   Complete the table to show how much water you think you use in one day.

Water usage	Quantities used
flushing the toilet	
drinking water	
washing hands	
having a shower/bath	
washing up	
cleaning	
other	

2   Look at the following questions. What do you think the answers are?

a   How much total water do you think you use a day? _____

b   How much water do you think the average person needs every day? _____

c   What percentage of the world's population is without clean drinking water? _____

d   What diseases can people get if they don't have clean drinking water? _____

3   What ways do you keep yourself clean every day? For each way you keep yourself clean, give a reason why you do it.

Example: *Brush my teeth – breath can get smelly, avoid gum disease, etc.*

_____

_____

_____

_____

_____

_____

4   Here are some answers to the questions in Activity C2. Match the answer to the question number.

Diarrhoea and cholera ☐

20–50 litres ☐

11% ☐

5   Read the facts below to check you matched the correct answer and question.

Water facts

The UN suggests that each person needs 20–50 litres of water a day to ensure their basic needs for drinking, cooking and cleaning.
(Source: World Water Assessment Programme, WWAP)

In 2010, 89% of the world's population, or 6.1 billion people, used improved drinking water sources, exceeding the MDG target (88%); 92% are expected to have access in 2015. By 2015, 67% will have access to improved sanitation facilities (the MDG target is 75%).
(Source: WHO)

11% of the global population, or 783 million people, are still without access to improved sources of drinking water.
(Source: JMP 2012)

Globally, diarrhoea is the leading cause of illness and death, and 88% of diarrhoeal deaths are due to a lack of access to sanitation facilities, together with inadequate availability of water for hygiene and unsafe drinking water.
(Source: JMP)

Washing hands with soap can reduce the risk of diarrhoeal diseases by up to 47%.
(Source: WHO)

Overall, the number of cholera cases for the decade 2000–10 increased by 130%.
(Source: WHO, 2010)

With increasing populations living in peri-urban slums and refugee camps, as well as increasing numbers of people exposed to the impacts of humanitarian crises, the risk from cholera will likely increase worldwide.
(Source: WWDR, 2012)

Adapted from: www.unwater.org

67

6 Using the information on page 67, say if the following are true or false.

   a Fifty litres of water a day is normally the maximum a person would need to use.

   b The percentage of improved drinking sources is predicted to worsen.

   c By 2015, more people will have improved access to better sanitation than drinking sources.

   d 11% of the world population is the same as 783 million people.

   e Diarrhoea is the main cause of death internationally.

   f A simple solution to diarrhoea is to wash your hands with soap.

   g Cholera is on the decline.

   h Cholera is affected by people's living conditions.

D Reading and writing

1 In the Coursebook, you prepared a presentation on a water item. Look at the presentation slide below on the 'shadoof' and make three notes about the information.

Example: *shadoof – Arabic word*

What is a 'shadoof'?

Today I'm going to talk about a 'shadoof', which is an irrigation tool. 'Shadoof' is an Arabic word and is more commonly known in English as a 'well pole'.

The 'shadoof' was originally developed in ancient Egypt and images of it exist from as far back as around 2000 BCE. It is still used in many areas of Africa and Asia to draw water.

2 Use your notes from Activity D1 and the information below to write a paragraph (80–100 words) about the 'shadoof'.

Use / raise water / one level to another

Operated by hand

One end pole / other end weight

Egyptians built canals / improve irrigation / more land needed water

Bucket filled with water / weight raised bucket

Still used today / Egypt / Near East

Over 2500 litres / per day

Maximum water depth / 3 metres

Bucket animal skin / 20 litres water

Unit 14: How important is oil?

A Vocabulary

1 **In each of the word lists below, underline the odd one out. Give a reason for your choice.**

Example: *who   what   <u>did</u>   where*

> *They are all question words, but with 'did'; the answer is 'yes' or 'no'.*

a glasses   credit card   table   phone

_____

b taxi   police car   ambulance   fire engine

_____

c whale   dolphin   seal   octopus

_____

d smaller   more efficient
more popular   more energetic

_____

e pad   pencil   book   pen

_____

f email   SMS   fax   apps

_____

g planned   painted   lost   dialled

_____

h currently   presently   now   formerly

_____

i lens   eye   glasses   audio

_____

j circle   oval   round   wheel

_____

2 **Put the words in the correct order to make a sentence.**

a daily important is in how oil to us lives our?

_____

b manufactured many oil are items made from.

_____

c many are seriously because plastic injured animals of litter.

_____

d how used barrels of many daily oil are?

_____

e the 1983 mobile was the sold first public in to phone.

_____

f convenience mobile were than more status of a phones symbol a.

_____

g number smaller when should a is ten or we word write the.

_____

h glasses one developed eye from frame lens in a just.

_____

i some say important the people is invention the most wheel.

_____

j modern the lens old is 120 contact years.

_____

3 Use the words in the box to complete the sentences below.

> extent   moulded   ivory   emigrated
> invention   versatile   oven   rocketed
> widespread   synthetic   decades

a The _____ of the phone revolutionised people's lives.

b The sweets tasted so _____ that even the children couldn't eat them.

c The _____ to which people speak English as a Second Language is vast.

d Pizza tastes much better if cooked in a clay _____ .

e Measles have become _____ again because people have chosen not to vaccinate.

f Rice is a very _____ grain, as it can be used with anything.

g The pots are _____ by hand and so each one is different.

h The prices _____ when it was seen how popular the apps were.

i People have been driving for _____ now and will never give up the car.

j Many people _____ from Ireland when there was a potato famine.

k Many elephants have been killed for their tusks to supply the _____ market.

B Language focus: Question forms, tenses with time references

Question forms

1 Match the question with the answer, then practise reading it.

What time does the film start?	Nobody famous. There are some unknown names.
How much do the tickets cost?	I'll give it to you. It's www …
Who are the actors?	There is a show at 18.00 and again at 20.30.
Why didn't they use anyone famous?	We'll put the information on our website.
When does the next film come out?	It should be here next week.
How will I find out?	It depends. If you're an adult $8 and $6 if you're a child.
Where can I get the address from?	Don't know. Suppose it was cheaper.

2 Now complete the dialogue by writing the questions for the answers below.

a Who _____?

All the teachers and classes.

b When _____?

It's next week.

c What _____?

I think 19.30, but you'd better check.

d Who's _____?

Well, every class has to do something. I think our class is bringing the cakes.

e Why _____?

I think because it's the school's anniversary. It's ten years old!

f Are _____?

How _____?

Yes, I think so. It won't be much – about $5.

g Where _____?

In the sports' hall, because it's nice and big.

h How _____?

I'll get my dad to take me. Do you want to come with us?

Tenses with time references

3 **What tense (or tenses) is usually used with each of the time references below?**

Example: *Many years ago = past simple*

a Since. _____

b Today. _____

c Last week. _____

d Last night. _____

e Come now! _____

f At the weekend. _____

g The month before last. _____

h This week. _____

i Presently. _____

j The day before yesterday. _____

k Lately. _____

l After. _____

m Yet. _____

4 **Use time references to write complete sentences about yourself.**

Example: *I used to wear glasses many years ago, but now I wear contact lenses.*

a _____ since we last joined.

b Last week, _____ .

c _____ since last night.

d Come now! _____ .

e _____ at the weekend.

f _____ the month before last.

g _____ this week.

h _____ the day before yesterday.

i _____ lately

j _____ yet.

C Reading

1 **The words and phrases below all appear in the text you are going to read. Use paper or digital reference sources to check their meaning.**

> cruising altitude   founded   tirelessly
> predecessor   flying saucer   altitudes
> gained   fins and pods   120 horsepower
> hazard   feasible   parachute   viable

2 **Read the text on the next page. Find a word or phrase that has a similar meaning to each of the following. Use a dictionary to help you.**

a congestion (paragraph 1)

_____

b vision (1)

_____

c people you work with (2)

_____

d very intelligent people (2)

_____

e information (3)

_____

f unusual (4)

_____

g predictions, guesses (4)

_____

h break down (5)

_____

i possible (7)

_____

The Moller M400 Skycar

[1] Imagine this: your daily trip to the office at 500 kilometres per hour with no traffic jams, no roadworks and a cruising altitude of 10,000 metres. Sounds like science fiction? Well, not for much longer – thanks to one man's idea.

[2] Moller International was founded in 1983 by Dr Paul Moller, a Canadian-born US engineer, to produce personal vertical take-off and landing aircraft (VTOL). His colleagues said it couldn't be done, but, like many geniuses, Dr Moller worked tirelessly towards his dream: a personal flying car that could take off from any back garden or street and be as easy to fly as a car is to drive, if not easier.

[3] In 1989, Moller produced the Skycar's predecessor, the M200x. This looked like a flying saucer, and the pilot sat in the middle. Moller has flown the M200x over 150 times at altitudes up to 15 metres. Its speed is slow and, therefore, not very practical for long-distance travel. However, the knowledge gained from this project was put to good use for the M400.

[4] The M400 itself certainly looks like something from a sci-fi movie – a mixture of fins and pods that would not look out of place in *Bladerunner*. The power for the vehicle comes from eight small 120-horsepower Rotapower engines. The Rotapower engines will allow the M400 Skycar to fly at 500 kilometres per hour, with a 1500-kilometre range, although future projections show that it could give a better performance. One of the best things about the lightweight engine is that it causes far less pollution than a regular engine.

[5] Some driver/pilot training will be necessary. Removing the hazard of untrained drivers makes the

Skycar more feasible, but there are still many worries about safety. With eight engines, if one or two do not work, the Skycar will still stay in the air, and if a computer breaks, there are still two more. There will even be a parachute for landing when systems fail, but what happens when a Skycar comes down in a crowded city street?

[6] Moller predicts ten-metre diameter 'vertiports' on top of city buildings where Skycars will be able to land and take off. As for overcrowding, according to Moller, even if there were the same number of Skycars in the sky tomorrow as there are cars on the roads today, each Skycar in the sky would be nearly 2 kilometres away (in all directions) from any other Skycar in the sky.

[7] Your own personal Skycar may seem like a dream at the moment, but Dr Moller's work and the technology now available make it an increasingly viable option, so watch the skies!

Adapted from www.21stcentury.co.uk

3 Read the text again, then copy and complete the notes below.

The Moller M400 Skycar

Moller's company set up in **(a)** _____ .

VTOL = **(b)** _____ .

M200x made in **(c)** _____ .

Main problem with M200x is **(d)** _____ .

M400 gets power from **(e)** _____ and it can travel at speeds up to **(f)** _____ with a **(g)** _____ of 1500 kilometres.

M400 engines produce less **(h)** _____ than normal car engines.

City buildings may provide **(i)** _____ for Skycars in the future.

Little chance of overcrowding because **(j)** _____ .

D Reading and writing

1   Look at the passage *The Moller M400 Skycar* again. Would you say the text was:

- objective?
- persuasive?
- entertaining?

The first paragraph is *persuasive*, as it makes the Skycar sound unique and amazing. Find the word *geniuses* and *worked tirelessly* in the second paragraph. Again, these give a positive feel to the article and persuade you of the idea.

Find some more examples of words or phrases in the article that are positive and persuasive.

_____

_____

_____

_____

2   Complete the table with different types of food. Then think of an adjective to describe each type of food.

Food you like	pasta			
Adjectives	delicious			
Food you don't like				
Adjectives				
Food you have to eat				
Adjectives				

3   Imagine you didn't like the idea of the Moller M400 Skycar. Write a newspaper report of about 80 words to explain how you feel. Use adjectives to describe your feelings. A few sentences have been done to get you started.

Dr Paul Moller, a Canadian-born US engineer, believes he is developing a vehicle of the future, where getting from A to B will be free of stress and hindrances. His idea is the dream of science-fiction films and likely to be just that – a dream.

_____

_____

_____

_____

_____

_____

73

Unit 15: How do you say 'bridge' in your language?

A Vocabulary

1 Look at the words and phrases in the grid, then write them next to the correct definition below.

story	quaint	backward	period	contemporaries
millennium	hunters	natural disaster	reception	uncivilised
entire	igloo	crashing torrent	bridge	creation
chapel	philosopher	rushing rapids	settlers	chaos

a a thousand years _____

b tale, narrative _____

c formation _____

d era, age _____

e old-fashioned _____

f timid, reluctant _____

g not cultured _____

h whole _____

i ice house _____

j flyover _____

k small church _____

l welcome desk _____

m colonisers _____

n food seekers _____

o theorist _____

p from the same era _____

q disorder _____

r fast-flowing water _____

s environmental tragedy _____

t destructive flow _____

2 Which two alphabets can you identify in the grid?

α	β	γ	δ	ε	ζ	η	θ	ι	κ	λ	μ	ν	ξ	ο	π	ρ	σ	τ	υ	φ	χ	ψ	ω		
a	b	c	d	e	f	g	h	i	j	k	l	m	n	o	p	q	r	s	t	u	v	w	x	y	z

3 Use the code grid above to complete these sentences with words from Activity A1.

a They live in a ρ φ α ι ξ υ little house in a village near London.

_____

b The θ φ ξ υ ε σ τ walked all day in the forest until they found some game.

_____

c They celebrated the ν ι μ μ ε ξ ξ ι φ ν with a big party.

_____

d ξαυφσαμ διτατυεστ seem to be a more regular occurrence with global warming.

_____

e The εξυισε class went on a school trip to the mountains.

_____

f The σεγεπυιοξ should always be staffed by two people throughout the day.

_____

g The river became a γσατθιξη υοσσεξυ after the heavy rains of the season.

_____

h The President and his γοξυενποσασιετ are of a younger age than previous generations.

_____

4 **Write the following numbers as words.**

Example: *244 m – two hundred and forty-four metres*

a 1377 m _____   **e** 1982 _____

b 5850 m _____   **f** 50,080,310 _____

c 2004 _____   **g** 67,356 _____

d 1894 _____   **h** 1,372,896 _____

B Language focus: Verbs ending in -*en*, intensifying adjectives

Verbs ending in -*en*

1 **Choose the correct answer from the options given below each question.**

a The fruit needs to _____ because it is too hard to eat.

A *soft*   B *soften*   C *softly*

b We need to _____ her up, as she is very weak after her illness.

A *strengthen*   B *strength*   C *strong*

c The puppy is very _____ because he's not had any water for days.

A *weak*   B *weaken*   C *weakly*

d They should use _____ water when they wash up, as it's wasteful.

A *lessen*   B *less*   C *least*

e She took a sip of water to _____ her throat.

A *moist*   B *moisten*   C *moisture*

f The little girl smiled at her aunt _____ when she gave her a kiss.

  A sweet   B sweetly   C sweeten

g The fruit on the trees quickly _____ in the warm sunshine.

  A ripened   B ripe   C ripen

h The sky was soon _____ and it was a sign that bad weather was coming.

  A darken   B dark   C darkness

2 **Complete the sentences below using the words and pictures. You will need to add -*en* to some words.**

strength	quiet	bright	loose	thick	children	tree	sky
soup	shirt	trousers	door	milk	fast	wide	length

a The _____ need to _____ down, as they're very noisy.

b You need to _____ those _____ , as they're too short.

c That _____ is very tight on the neck, _____ it!

d That _____ does look very nice. I think you should _____ it a bit, though.

e You need to _____ that door frame, otherwise the _____ won't fit.

f If you drink _____ when you're a child, it will _____ your bones.

g _____ the dog to the _____ and then it won't run away.

h The day will _____ later, as the forecast is a clear _____ .

Intensifying adjectives

3   Imagine you visited one of the bridges discussed in the Coursebook. You send a postcard to your friend, describing an experience you had when you were there.

Complete the postcard. Use the intensifying adjectives in the box to fill the gaps on the left, then fill in the name and address details for your friend.

| absolute | ultimate | total | utter | entire | complete |

Hi _____

Had the _____ experience when I visited London recently, as went to see Tower Bridge. It was an _____ pleasure to see it for real, as have always seen it in pictures only. I did the _____ tour of the place and walked around in _____ disbelief, as it's such a cool bridge. The mechanics of the place are an _____ dream for an engineer, and I got the man who worked there to explain the _____ system to me.

Tell you more later.

_____
(full name)

_____
(house number and street name)

_____
(area of street)

_____
(town)

_____
(code)

_____
(country)

C   Reading

1   You are going to read a text about bionic buildings. Match each word or phrase from the text on page 78 with a suitable definition.

Word or phrase from the text	Definition
array	aims
curved	collection
goals	copies
harbour	does not destroy the environment
high-rise buildings	higher on one side
lagoon	path of a railway
mimics	pollution
sloping	port, marina
smog	rounded
sustainable	small lake
tracks	very tall structures, skyscrapers

2 Read the text carefully, then fill in the gaps, using the words and phrases from Activity C1.

Amazing bionic buildings

Bionic architecture

Have you ever pictured what the **(a)** _____ of the future might look like? Well, bionic architecture ignores the traditional buildings that we've been used to for so long. Instead, it takes its design ideas from the **(b)** _____ lines of biological structures and the natural world. The result is an **(c)** _____ of some of the most amazing buildings, and some of the smartest – the designs are based on clever mathematical and biological calculations. So, let's look at some of the most incredible examples of bionic architecture and some of the leading bionic architects in the world.

The Anti-smog Building

This is one of the projects from Vincent Callebaut, a young French architect in the world of bionic architecture. It's a mixed-use building, built over old railway **(d)** _____ in Paris. A natural **(e)** _____ , as well as views of Paris, are both bonuses that make people want to spend time in this eco-friendly building, which is designed using green technologies that actually remove the **(f)** _____ from the Paris air.

The Ascent at Roebling Bridge

This building was constructed by Daniel Libeskind and it reflects the architect's **(g)** _____ in relation to bionic architecture. The **(h)** _____ roof takes design ideas from the natural environment and also offers residents of the building a wonderful view of the city. The natural tones of the building were specifically chosen to reflect the earth and sky of the area.

The Urban Cactus

This is a 19-storey residential building, shaped like an irregular pattern of outdoor spaces. Natural sunlight and a unique design on the **(i)** _____ give it the feeling of bionic architecture. However, it's not 100 per cent green, nor is it **(j)** _____ ; therefore, it is not mentioned on most bionic architecture lists.

The Treescraper Tower of Tomorrow

As the name suggests, this is a skyscraper that has been designed in a way that **(k)** _____ the growth and change of a tree. A curved, aerodynamic building, it uses minimal construction materials, while making maximum use of the enclosed space. All of the water in the building is recycled in a way similar to how a tree would reuse water and nutrients. Waste water flows into the building's three gardens, and the water from the gardens is reused in the toilets. It uses solar electricity and is made completely of recyclable materials.

Adapted from http://scribol.com

3 Answer these questions.

a Which building is not completely bionic?

_____

b Which buildings make use of water in their design?

_____

c From which buildings can you get a good view?

_____

d Which building specifically reduces air pollution?

_____

D Reading and writing

1 Look at this newspaper headline.

Stunned victim turns hero!

Write a short paragraph explaining what you think the story is about. Include all the words and phrases below.

children	school excursion	1-35W Mississippi bridge
collapse	back door	2007 Mr Hernandez hospitalisation

_____

_____

_____

_____

_____

2 Here are the phrases that go with the words above. Match the two parts, then rewrite your paragraph.

a 61 in the bus with adults. _____

b Tired and on their way home from water park. _____

c While they were being driven over it. _____

d Summer programme's sports coordinator. _____

e Eight-lane, steel. _____

f Summer. _____

g Kicked open and passed kids out. _____

h Only 16 needed. _____

_____

_____

_____

_____

_____

_____

3 **Read the real story of what happened.**

> **Stunned victim turns hero!**
>
> Sixty-one children and adults on their way back from a summer-school excursion to a water park were being taken home. They were quiet and tired, with some still wearing their swimming costumes, when suddenly, the bus they were in was hanging over the edge of a bridge, which had suddenly collapsed while they were being driven over it. One minute there they were, happy and tired after an exciting day, and the next hanging over the edge of a bridge in a bus in danger of falling into the mighty Mississippi River.
>
> The route? The 1-35W Mississippi eight-lane steel bridge which, in the summer of 2007, suddenly collapsed, taking many people with it. But, for the children in the bus, their hero was their summer programme's sports coordinator, Mr Hernandez, who, just following his instincts, kicked open the back entrance of the bus and got the kids out. The children were quickly handed to people outside, with the clock ticking and the river waiting to swallow them up. But, because of Mr Hernandez's quick thinking, all the children were saved and only 16 needed hospitalisation.

4 **Now match your paragraph with the newspaper article. How is your story different to the original story? Complete the table to show the differences.**

My story	The original story
In my story, the ...	

Unit 16: Where are the Seven Wonders of the Ancient World?

A Vocabulary

1   The names of the Seven Wonders are mixed up opposite. Cross out the incorrect name at the end of each and write the correct one.

a   The Temple of Rhodes.   _____

b   The Statue of Alexandria.   _____

c   The Great Pyramid of Artemis.   _____

d   The Lighthouse of Babylon.   _____

e   The Mausoleum of Zeus.   _____

f   The Hanging Gardens of Halicarnassus.   _____

g   The Colossus of Giza.   _____

2   **Which of the Seven Wonders is being described in each of the statements below?**

a   This was built 4500 years ago and is one of the oldest in its area; it still stands.

_____

b   This was destroyed by an earthquake 2100 years ago and built to please a wife in the area of present-day Iraq.

_____

c   This took 120 years to build and then it was burnt down! It was located in present-day Turkey.

_____

d   This was 12 metres tall and made of ivory and gold plating.

_____

e   This was a grand tomb to remember somebody, although the Crusaders did not want this.

_____

f   This was believed to welcome and protect anybody who went there.

_____

g   This was not a pyramid, although it was nearly as tall as one.

_____

3 Look at Activity F2 in your Coursebook. Complete the sentences below using a word or phrase from either Section A, B, C or D in the table on page 133.

a Section A: The shop was very close: just a _____ from the school.

b Section D: The _____ building could be clearly seen in the distance.

c Section A: At night, the quiet town became very _____ and full of activity.

d Section C: Markets are wonderful places for finding _____ and other small items.

e Section C: They often went for a _____ the Corniche as the sun went down.

f Section D: A great meal is sometimes described as a _____ .

g Section A: The sound of birds _____ loudly means it's probably time to wake up!

h Section B: The shout of 'Run!' had people _____ in all directions.

i Section D: We had a really _____ experience – everything was perfect, just as we wanted it to be.

j Section A: When traffic is _____ there is just no point in getting frustrated.

k Section C: The noise from the _____ shouting out their prices was deafening.

l Section B: Living in a fishing port means that we can see the _____ whenever we want.

B **Language focus: *is thought/said/believed*, etc., compound nouns and complex noun phrases**

is thought/said/believed, etc.

1 Remember how the 'reporting' or 'impersonal' form of the passive is formed: using a structure e.g. *thought*, followed by *to + have been* + past participle (v3). Complete the paragraph about Petra in Jordan below, using the passive and the following verbs.

say	think	believe	claim	report

The word 'Petra' comes from the Greek to mean 'stone' and is a historical and archaeological city in Jordan. It is also now one of the Seven Modern Wonders of the World, as well as a World Heritage Site since 1985. It was carved into the wall of a desert canyon and is also **(a)** _____ (*give*) the name 'Rose City' due to the colour of the stone from which it is hewn. It was **(b)** _____ (*establish*) around 320 BCE by the Nabataeans, who were ancient Arabs from North Arabia. In its heyday, Petra **(c)** _____ (*fortify*) as a fort, a port of call in the spice trade, but, most importantly, a supplier of water due to its exploitation of the water supply in the region. At its peak, an estimated 30,000 people lived there, but then it was **(d)** _____ (*destroy*) in the 4th century by an earthquake. This devastated its water system and, along with the change in trade routes, led to its decline. The city **(e)** _____ (*abandon*) in 1189 and remained unknown to the Western world until 1812, when it was discovered by a Swiss explorer.

2 **Rewrite each sentence, so that the meaning stays the same, using *is thought/said/believed*.**

a People know that the thief has been robbing other houses in the street.

The thief _____

_____ .

b It is estimated that many marine animals have been killed in badly placed fishing nets.

Many marine animals _____

_____ .

c Everyone thought that the painting had been destroyed in the fire.

The painting _____

_____ .

d People know that many beautiful buildings have been destroyed by earthquakes.

Beautiful buildings _____

_____ .

e Everyone thought the painting had been stolen before the exhibition.

The painting _____

_____ .

f The two men are thought to have been injured while climbing the mountain.

They are _____

_____ .

Compound nouns and complex noun phrases

3 **Complete these sentences with noun clauses.**

Example: *He feels tired. It's not surprising he feels tired.*

a She has resigned from her job. It's a shame _____

_____ .

b You don't want me to come. It's upsetting _____

_____ .

c You are feeling much better. I'm glad _____

_____ .

d She's upset. I'm sorry _____

_____ .

e She didn't get the scholarship. She told me _____

_____ .

f It's a good price for children. He believes _____

_____ .

g You're leaving. He has guessed _____

_____ .

h She's been very silly. She agrees _____

_____ .

C Reading

1 **The train called the Orient-Express is part of our heritage and history, just like the New7Wonders you learnt about in the Coursebook. You are going to read a text about this train. Look at these phrases. In which section do you think you will find them? Write the letter next to the phrases.**

Sections:

A *Carriage* **C** *History*

B *Dining* **D** *Life on board*

a afternoon tea ☐

b cosy confines ☐

c French silverware ☐

d panoramic views ☐

e personal steward ☐

f romance, adventure and pleasure ☐

g Sleeping Car 3309 ☐

h snowdrifts ☐

83

2 **Skim the text below. Choose a heading from Activity C1 for each of the four sections. Then read the text again and check your answers.**

The legendary Venice Simplon-Orient-Express

[1] _____

Romance, adventure and pleasure are all intimately bound up in journeys that criss-cross Europe between some of the world's most alluring cities. Bombed, shot at and marooned in snowdrifts, the Orient-Express has a history that is both legendary and colourful.

[2] _____

Each of the carriages, which today form the famous Venice Simplon-Orient-Express, has a history of its own, with long years of service criss-crossing the frontiers of Europe, operating for a variety of railway companies. The carriages have taken on characters of their own, as intriguing as the characters of those who travelled within their cosy confines.

The continental carriages have always been identified by numbers – these inconspicuous numbers, however, conceal a thick plot of history and intrigue. Sleeping Car 3309, for example, was part of the service which, in 1929, was stuck in a snowdrift for ten days, 60 miles outside Istanbul, along with a full complement of passengers, who survived only with the assistance of nearby Turkish villagers. Sleeping Car 3425 was part of the Orient-Express service used by King Carol of Romania. Some Orient-Express carriages also saw active service during the Second World War, either because they were taken over by the German Army, or because they were used by the US Transportation Corps.

[3] _____

Step aboard the Venice Simplon-Orient-Express and you step back into a more gracious, more elegant age. Your personal steward, instantly available to attend to your every comfort, will show you to your compartment of gleaming wood, polished brass, soft towels and crisp linen. Your comfortable compartment is a restful retreat offering panoramic views of ever-changing landscapes.

[4] _____

Your meals on board will be unforgettable. Set the tone with a visit to the Bar Car, famous for its delicious cocktails and welcoming atmosphere. Then move on to one of our three dining cars, where softly muted lighting enhances the mood, while fine linen, French silverware and heavy crystal invite you to prepare for a meal to remember. All dishes are freshly prepared on board by French chefs, with the finest supplies taken on board during the train's journey.

Lunch, dinner and brunch are served by the Italian waiters in one of the three individually styled Restaurant Cars: Lalique, Etoile du Nord or Chinoise, and breakfast and afternoon tea are served in passengers' compartments.

Table d'hôte meals are included in the fare, while an _à la carte_ menu and 24-hour compartment service is available additionally. The _Maître d'_ will come to your cabin to take your lunch and dinner reservations.

Adapted from www.orient-express.com

3 **Answer these questions.**

a How do you know that the carriages have been used for a long time? Give **two** reasons.

_____

_____

b Which **four** nationalities, which **two** countries and which **one** continent are mentioned in the text?

_____

_____

c Which date is given in the text? What happened on this date?

_____

_____

d **Five** different meals are served on the train. What are they?

_____

_____

e Give **four** negative events that the Orient-Express has suffered.

_____

_____

f Name **three** materials that you will see in your compartment.

_____

_____

g Where are meals served on the train? Give **four** different places.

_____

_____

D Reading and writing

1 Imagine a friend is coming to visit your country from abroad. In your notebook, make a list of places they could visit and what they can do in each place, in a table like this one. Name at least five places.

Name of place to visit	Things to do there

2 Give some advice about each of the places you have mentioned.

Example: *Colosseum, Rome*
If you visit the Colosseum in Rome, make sure you wear comfortable shoes, as there is a lot of walking about and standing in queues.

_____

_____

_____

_____

_____

_____

_____

3   Now look at this newspaper article about Machu Picchu. Imagine you are going to visit this famous site with a friend. Think of what you want to do there and make a list. Make suggestions to give to your friend, so you can plan your trip.

Machu Picchu: Trip of a lifetime

Machu Picchu is so well known, and so certain to fill travellers with high expectations, that you might think it's doomed to disappoint. No other South American archaeological site comes close when it comes to visitor numbers and broad appeal (coach tourists mingle with backpackers and hard-core hikers at the ruin every day of the year). Only Sacsayhuamán in Cuzco – which is usually part of a Machu Picchu itinerary – is comparable for sheer scale and architectural audacity.

But, with a bit of careful planning and the right approach, you will find the site as enchanting and engaging as any on the planet. The draw of Machu Picchu (which means 'old mountain' in the Quechua language) is obvious: a 550-year-old citadel built by the most advanced – and, in Peru, the very last – pre-Columbian society in the spectacular setting of a saddle between two forest-clad Andean peaks that has been preserved enough to be recognisable as a city. It is high: 2430 metres above sea level.

It is large: the ruins are the size of a village and, combined with an adjoining forest and wilderness park, the 'historical sanctuary', as UNESCO describes it, covers more than 300 square kilometres. It is also mysterious: we know its functions were partly residential and partly religious, but we are still guessing about its cosmic positioning and its academic importance to the Incas.

Machu Picchu is set in humid subtropical forests, providing a protected habitat for ferns and palms and several endangered species, notably the spectacled bear. Add in swirling clouds, llamas grazing on the terraces and the option to arrive following a hike on mountain trails and/or a train trip through the valley of the Urubamba River (aka the 'Sacred Valley'), and you have a memorable trip that can last two, seven or 14 days. You just have to work out how to catch that quiet moment at the 'hitching post of the sun' and find the right angle for a tourist-free photograph.

Adapted from www.telegraph.co.uk

Unit 17: What impact does fashion have on teenagers?

A Vocabulary

1 **Match each of the pictures with the correct sentence.**

The girl's hats are very beautiful.

The girls' hats are very beautiful.

2 **Add an apostrophe to make the following sentences correct.**

a I went to my sister-in-laws house. (singular house and sister)

b I went to my sisters-in-laws houses. (plural houses and sisters)

c Mr Joness shoes are too big for him.

d Monroe and Charles house is in Zanzibar.

e Its a very hot day, so be careful of the sun.

f You should always dot your is in a sentence.

g Childrens clothes are on the first floor.

h This is my cousins favourite uncle.

3 **Some of the words in italics have been used in the wrong sentences. Cross out where the words are incorrect and write the correct ones.**

a You can *monitored* if a person is lying by their heart rate. _____

b I prefer the original *fabric* of the song. _____

c The suitcase is so *version* it won't be heavy to carry. _____

d She should be *incorporated* at all times until her temperature falls.

_____

e These jeans are highly *wearable* and washable. _____

f The milk and eggs should be *embedded* together in the cake mixture.

_____

g The car is not only *aesthetically* pleasing, but also an engineering miracle.

_____

h *Civilian* and military personnel are all invited to the grand opening.

_____

i A thorn was *diagnosed* in his foot and he couldn't walk. _____

j If you *generate* your handwriting, I'll be able to read it! _____

k He was *detect* with diabetes when he was only 11! _____

87

l *Blending* the two colours gives a softer shade. _____

m The sofa is made of *lightweight* and gets dirty easily. _____

n They could *improve* more income by working more. _____

4 **Now match these 14 definitions with the words from Activity A3.**

a can be worn _____

b check something regularly _____

c cloth or material _____

d combined with _____

e create _____

f detect _____

g get better _____

h identify an illness _____

i mixing together _____

j non-military _____

k placed inside _____

l specific variety _____

m weighing less than expected _____

n appealingly _____

B Language focus: Word building, modal verbs

Word building

1 **Identify the words in italics as an adjective, noun, verb or adverb and write them in the correct column of the table on page 89.**

a He was famous while he lived, but then died in *obscurity*.

b If water is added to the mixture, it will *instantaneously* harden.

c To put it *mildly*, he is lazy and won't pass his exams at the rate he is going.

d There is a feeling of *permanence* about this place; it just never changes.

e She is normally a *sociable* person, but tonight she is very quiet.

f If you mix it just *slightly*, then it won't damage it.

g He *ambitiously* pursued his dream to become a politician.

h They have had to *widen* the road due to the volume of traffic.

Adjective	Noun	Verb	Adverb
obscure	obscurity	to obscure	obscurely

2 Complete the table by writing the missing forms of each word. You may not be able to fill in all the gaps.

Modal verbs

3 Look at this statement from a text about film and music piracy. Which is the modal verb? Which is the main verb? Underline them.

Downloading tunes from the Internet may be a great new way to buy your music …

4 What does the modal do to the main verb? What is its function?

_____

_____

5 Are the following statements about modal verbs true or false?

a *Can*, *could*, *should* and *will* are also examples of modal verbs. _____

b You don't use an *s* in third person singular.

_____

c They are followed directly by the infinitive of another verb. _____

d They can refer to deduction, probability, certainty or speculation. _____

e Modal verbs can be conjugated like other verbs.

_____

f They modify the meaning of another verb in the sentence. _____

6 Complete the sentences with *should've* / *shouldn't have* / *have to* / *might* / *must* / *may* / *can't* / *ought* / *could* / *will* and the correct form of a verb from the box.

> open   leave   help   cook   study
> borrow   offer   walk   be (2)

a I _____ _____ _____ to babysit.

b I _____ _____ _____ her across the road.

c I _____ _____ harder for this exam.

d _____ I _____ the window please? I'm so hot!

e I _____ _____ any more, I'm so tired.

f _____ I _____ a pencil, please?

g My keys _____ _____ in my bag.

h I _____ _____ able to make it, but it's getting very late.

i Sorry, I _____ _____ _____ now, as my bus leaves in ten minutes.

j I _____ _____ if you do the washing up!

89

C Reading and writing

1   Read the description of the photograph and identify the different people that are being described.

This photograph shows a family that perhaps originates from eastern Europe. The photograph would have been taken around the middle of the 20th century. It looks like quite a mixed family with different generations.

The couple in the middle may be the grandparents of the little boys sitting on their laps, as well as some of the other children, who could be cousins. The woman on the right at the back could be the mother of the teenage girl and boy on her right. The two women on either side of the middle row could be aunts of the younger people or perhaps the mothers of the younger people.

The older couple are wearing clothes that are quite traditional. The headscarf that the old woman is wearing could suggest that she is from a country such as Russia. The family does not appear to be very wealthy, as their clothes are quite simple and practical. The younger people are wearing quite normal clothes, ones that are similar to those worn today, apart from the women's dresses perhaps.

2   **Find an old photograph showing people from your country and write a description (80–100 words) of the people in it.**

_____

_____

_____

_____

_____

_____

_____

_____

_____

_____

Unit 18: What does that sign mean?

A Vocabulary

1 Look at the passage below. Write out words to replace the signs.

> The other day I 🚶 down the street and couldn't remember the way, so I asked 👩 and she told me to ↖. I was looking for the 🚗 but, because many of the roads were ⊖, I was having a real problem finding it. Also, some of the roads were 🚳 and I had my pet with me. I was hungry, so thought I would stop @ 🍴 and have a bite to eat. I then needed 🚻 and was ready to try again. This time, I thought I would ask a 👮 the way and soon I found my car. Well, by then I was late, as I had to get to the 🏥 to pick up my mother. I found a ♿ for her, as she was having problems walking. We went slowly to the car, going carefully over the ⚠, but the real problems were the 🛞, the 🛒 and the 👴 crossing the road. I did eventually get home, but had to stop @ the 📮 where there was 🚭, but people still were. When I got home, I 🧥 my coat and sat down for ☕ with my mother; we were both ready for 🛏.

_____

_____

_____

_____

_____

_____

_____

_____

_____

2 Complete the crossword. You can find all the words in Section F of your Coursebook.

Clues

Across

4 Very great (8)

5 A look on someone's face (10)

7 A small part of something (8)

8 Form of a language used from a particular area (7)

9 Clear expression of something (9)

10 A strong, regular repeated sound or movement (6)

11 Relating to someone's background (9)

Down

1 Human communication through the spoken or written form (8)

2 Developed or well-aged (6)

3 A choice (6)

4 Speech sounds (13)

6 The first or main one (7)

3 Now use forms of the words from the crossword to complete these sentences.

a He has excellent _____ and you wouldn't guess that he was from abroad.

b She misses her cat _____ and keeps looking for her.

c They have the _____ to come with us; it's not obligatory.

d The music has great _____ and makes you want to sing and dance.

e His face has a lot of _____ and he'd make a good actor.

f They speak a different _____ to us and I find it difficult to understand.

g The _____ source of carbohydrate for many countries is rice or potatoes.

h They learn about their _____ in a special class after school.

i They're quite _____ , but not adults yet.

j They're going to make a _____ on television tonight about the decision.

k It's interesting to study _____ because it helps you understand words you use.

l Only a _____ of the students want to go on the trip.

B Language focus: Position of adjectives, semi-fixed and fixed expressions

Position of adjectives

1 Underline the adjective in the following sentences. Say if it is predicative or attributive.

a The black window closed slowly._____

b This stretch of river is very dangerous. _____

c Michael feels ill._____

d A larger than necessary chocolate was given to the children. _____

e The blue sea is beautiful today. _____

f The man is old, but he's still able to be independent. _____

2 Complete each of the following sentences with a different adjective.

a She had a _____ smile when I greeted her.

b Her smile is _____ and lights up her face.

c He bought two _____ bread rolls.

d She gave him a bucket of _____ water for the plants.

e He put his hand in the water – the water was very _____ .

f They are a _____ family and do a lot together.

g The family appeared _____ as they got off the train after their trip.

h I saw lots of _____ clowns at the theatre that made me laugh.

Semi-fixed and fixed expressions

3 Correct the errors in these fixed expressions.

a You decide. It's up for you if you go.

_____

b What of the world do you mean by that?

_____

c Could you hold up a moment, please, while I change my shoes?

_____

d He's got mixed feelings with his new college.

_____

e Freeda feels very strong about doing so much homework.

_____

f She's so very pleased of her exam results.

_____

g That listens like a wonderful chance of a new experience.

_____

h Thank you as much for inviting us to your house.

_____

4 **Complete the sentences using a correct expression.**

a I'm good at learning languages, but _____ sciences.

b He _____ a mistake with his calculations in the maths exam.

c Can I _____ on this dress in size 12, please?

d Can I _____ you, madam? No, thank you, I'm just _____ .

e If you _____ me, you should buy it today.

f If you don't mind me _____ , that colour looks really nice on you.

g The way I _____ it, we've done all we can.

h You know _____ I think? She shouldn't go tonight.

C Reading

1 **You are going to read a text about how writing was created in the past. Before you read, use a dictionary or online references to check the meaning of the following words from the text.**

literally	fluid	constituent	track
concepts	civilisations	papyrus	
elided	scribes	scroll	

2 **Read the text below and complete each gap using a word or phrase from Activity C1.**

History of writing

Writing has its origins in two main **(a)** _____ , which, separately, were responsible for this totally transforming human development. These were Egyptian and the Sumerian (in what is now Iraq) and occurred about 3200 BCE.

Most early writing systems begin with small images used as words, **(b)** _____ depicting the thing in question. But pictograms of this kind are limited and some physical objects are too difficult to depict, as the words are **(c)** _____ rather than objects.

In about 3200 BCE, temple officials in Sumer develop a reliable and lasting method of keeping **(d)** _____ of the animals and other goods which are the temple's wealth. On lumps of wet clay, the scribes draw a simplified picture of the item in question. They then make a similar mark in the clay for the number counted and recorded. When allowed to bake hard in the sun, the clay tablet becomes a permanent document.

The second civilisation to develop writing, shortly after the Sumerians, is Egypt. The Egyptian characters are much more directly pictorial in kind than the Sumerian, but the system of suggesting objects and concepts is similar. The Egyptian characters are called hieroglyphs by the Greeks in about 500 BCE because, by that time, this form of writing is reserved for holy texts; hieros and glypho mean 'sacred' and 'engrave' in Greek.

Because of the importance of hieroglyphic inscriptions in temples and tombs, much of the creation of these beautiful characters is by painters, sculptors in relief and craftsmen modelling in plaster. But with the introduction of **(e)** _____ , the Egyptian script is also the business of **(f)** _____

The Egyptian scribe uses a fine reed pen to write on the smooth surface of the papyrus **(g)** _____ . Inevitably, the act of writing causes the hieroglyphs to become more **(h)** _____ than the strictly formal versions carved and painted in tombs.

In about 700 BCE, the pressure of business causes the Egyptian scribes to develop a more abbreviated version of the hieratic script. Its **(i)** _____ parts are still the same Egyptian hieroglyphs, established more than 2000 years previously, but they are now so **(j)** _____ that the result looks like an entirely new script. Known as demotic ('for the people'), it is harder to read than the earlier written versions of Egyptian.

Both hieroglyphs and demotic continue to be used until about 400 CE. Thereafter their secret is forgotten, until the chance discovery of the Rosetta Stone makes it possible for the hieroglyphic code to be cracked in the 19th century.

Bamber Gascoigne, HistoryWorld, History of Writing, www.historyworld.net/wrldhis/PlainTextHistories. asp?historyid=ab33

3 **Answer these questions.**

a What one single event brought about change in humankind?

_____

b Why was it that pictures or symbols alone were not effective?

_____

c How were records first kept?

_____

d What was different and similar about the Egyptian and Sumerian 'writing'?

_____

e How was the importance of writing hieroglyphics preserved?

_____

f How did the use of papyrus and a reed pen influence 'writing'?

_____

g What brought about a change in the style of writing and why?

_____

4 **Find the names of ten 'superheroes' in the word circle.**

catwomanspidermanthorbatmanwonderwomansupermanironmanincrediblehulkcaptainamericablackwidow

_____

_____

_____

_____

_____

_____

_____

_____

_____

_____

5 **How well do you know your superheroes? Which ones are being described below?**

a He comes from the planet Krypton. He wears red and blue with a red cape and a yellow letter across his chest. He can fly at supersonic speeds and possesses incredible strength.

_____

b He has a hammer disguised as a walking stick and is a thunder god. He can summon the elements of a storm, has incredible strength and a high resistance to physical injury.

_____

c A normal man, but a very clever mechanic, who builds suits that give him incredible powers of strength, flight and perception.

_____

d She is seen as a heroine fighting for justice, love, peace and women's equality. She has a wide range of superhuman powers and superior combat and battle skills.

_____

6 **Match the two parts to form a sentence.**

Superheroes became popular in the	more than real historic figures.
Some of them are known internationally	popularity for a while in the 1950s.
Numerous television shows, books and movies	life as a secretary.
Superman was	much more sophisticated.
Wonder Woman started	have been published and produced about them.
Superheroes did lose out in	when he came to television.
Batman became popular again in 1966	late 1930s and early 1940s.
Superheroes now make	the first comic book character.
The 2012 _Avengers_ film	has increased dramatically in recent years.
Demand for Superhero paraphernalia	was one of the most financially successful.
Superheroes have become	mistakes and have some human qualities.

Acknowledgements

The author and publishers are grateful for the permissions granted to reproduce texts in either the original or adapted form. While every effort has been made, it has not always been possible to identify the sources of the all materials used, or to trace all copyright holders. If any omissions are brought to our notice, we will be happy to include the appropriate acknowledgements on reprinting.

p. 9 adapted from *The Way Things Work* by David Macauley (Dorling Kindersley), copyright © Dorling Kinderley Ltd, text copyright © David Macauley, reproduced by permission of Penguin Books Ltd; p. 13 adapted from 'At 13,000 years, tree is world's oldest organism' by Steve Connor, *The Independent* (www.independent.co.uk), 22 December 2009. Reprinted by permission; p. 15 adapted from 'Can jumbos really paint?' by Desmond Morris, *Daily Mail*, 21 February 2009. Reprinted by permission; p. 19 adapted from 'Hurricane names: How are hurricanes named?', www.geology.com. Reprinted by permission; p. 20 adapted from 'Sri Lanka braces for more flooding', 12 December 2012, from www.abc.net.au. Copyright ABC 2012. Reprinted by permission; p. 24 adapted from www.mapsofworld.com, 13 July 2008. Reprinted by permission; p. 28 material adapted from www.travellersworldwide.com. Reprinted by permission; p. 29 material adapted from www.elrefugiodelburrito.com. Reprinted by permission; p. 33 adapted from 'Saving the wild orang-utan' by Reino Gevers. Reprinted by permission of Reino Gevers; p. 34 adapted from 'Weather – Nature's Forecasters – Animals and Birds' by Tree Change from http://treechange.hubpages.com. Reprinted by permission; pp. 37 and 38 adapted from *Study Skills & Strategies Success Guide* by M-C McInally and Eric Summers © 2005 M-C McInally and Eric Summer. Reprinted by permission of HarperCollins Publishers Ltd; p. 38 adapted from 'Usain Bolt vs. The Cheetah: Olympians of the Animal Kingdom', 30 July 2012, from www.livescience.com. Reprinted by permission of Wright's Media; p. 47 adapted from www.kidsastronomy.com, 18 July 2008. Reprinted by permission; p. 48 adapted from www.cavingintro.net. Reprinted by permission of Bob Robins; pp. 56–7 adapted from www.kidzworld.com, 21 July 2008. Reprinted by permission; p. 61 adapted from GrandAmericanAdventures.com, 22 July 2008. Reprinted by permission; p. 67 adapted from www.unwater.org. Reprinted by permission; p. 72 adapted from www.21stcentury.co.uk, 22 July 2008. Reprinted by permission; p. 78 adapted from '12 Most Amazing Bionic Buildings' from www.scribol.com. Reprinted by permission; p. 84 adapted from www.orient-express.com (now www.belmond.com), 24 July 2008. Reprinted by permission; p. 86 'Machu Picchu: Trip of a Lifetime' by Chris Ross, 20 September 2012, from *The Telegraph* © Telegraph Media Group Limited 2012. Reprinted by permission; pp. 93–4 adapted from HistoryWorld, History of Writing, http://www.historyworld.net/wrldhis/PlainTextHistories.asp?historyid=ab33. Reprinted by permission of Bamber Gascoigne.

All images courtesy of Shutterstock except p. 68 courtesy of Mary Evans Picture Library.

 Produced for Cambridge University Press by White-Thomson Publishing
+44 (0)843 208 7460
www.wtpub.co.uk

Project editor: Sonya Newland
Designer: Kim Williams, 320 Media
Illustrator: Steve Evans